Living *in the* Fullness *of* Jesus's Resurrection

FINDING FREEDOM IN ALL AREAS OF LIFE

JOANNA DUELL

ACKNOWLEDGMENTS

I would like to give a special thanks to my mother, Dondi Duell, for her constant encouragement for this book and her help in writing and editing. I would also like to give special thanks to Hannah Ahlfield for her wonderful help and support in the logistical details.

TABLE OF CONTENTS

INTRODUCTION

Jesus bought us so many wonderful things when He died and rose again on the cross. Through His Resurrection, He bought us salvation, but He then invited us into so much more! It doesn't matter if you are a brand-new Christian or have been a Christian for many years, the Lord invites you on this journey of discovering the depth of what He has made available to you.

Scripture details the many ways Jesus freed us from sin and death. Over the last few years, the Lord has highlighted to me in Scripture the many ways He has provided freedom, both in the smallest of ways and the ways He has given us freedom that go against what the world says we have to live with. He birthed in me a desire to teach others how to live in His fullness and how to experience all the freedom He bought for us. Jesus and the Holy Spirit have shown me and continue to show me through Scripture all the things we get to live in and how to experience those things in our lives. The Lord showed me through personal experience so much of His love and freedom, whether it was while I was working on college coursework, baking a new recipe, spending time soaking in His presence, or trying to get over a headache.

Jesus's heart is that we would learn to live in all the freedoms He bought for us on the cross. He desires for us to live triumphant lives that are not subject to sin and death. Jesus, Father God, and the Holy Spirit desire that we would walk in healing and freedom, whether it is from a cold, or a burn, or *anything* else.

I remember once, when I was baking in the kitchen, I needed to drain a pot of boiling water into the sink. There was another bowl in the sink as well. I dumped out the boiling water, but some of it got caught in the bowl, and I accidentally dipped my thumb into it. I instantly rebuked the burn because I believe we have been freed from every effect sin and death have over us— including sickness and damage to our bodies. I rebuked the burn and commanded it to heal instantly, have no blemish, and align under the freedom Jesus bought for me. Instantly, the burn left. There were no marks, no pain, no soreness, and no damage to the skin.

Jesus's desire is for us to live in the fullness of His Resurrection. Because of His Resurrection, we no longer have to be subject to the way the world functions, which aligns with the law of sin and death rather than with the law of the Spirit of life, which was instated by Jesus's Resurrection (Rom. 8:2). Through His Resurrection, Jesus broke the power of sin and death. He broke the power that sin and death gained when Adam and Eve sinned in the Garden of Eden. Jesus broke every effect that sin and death had over us.

Jesus invites us into a journey of discovering all that He has freed us from and all that He calls us into. Jesus invites us to live a life marked by Resurrection power. He invites us to change the way we think and to recognize all that He has given us to live in.

Paul teaches that our new life we have because of Jesus's Resurrection is meant to abound in glory. Glory, in the Greek, is a word that shows a transformation of your mind and a transformation in your physical life around you. This word also demonstrates a call to discovery and is characterized by pleasure, magnificence, and great beauty. This description is the type of new life we are called into by Jesus. His desire is to walk with us and for us to be transformed by His love. Jesus and the Holy Spirit want to show us all the wonderful things Jesus bought for us, but also to teach us how to live in them and to see them manifested in our lives.

As you read this book, you will be walked down a path that shows you how to interact with the heart of Jesus and how to see manifested the power of Jesus's Resurrection in your life. We will look at what He calls us into and how to open our hearts and minds to His new things for us. We will discover the depth of what He made available to us through His Resurrection, and we will walk into the wonderful freedom He designed for us to live in abundantly.

We are in a time where the Lord is fervently revealing His heart and is leading His people into a new era, when they will walk in the fullness of Jesus's Resurrection. The Lord has a deep desire for us to live in everything He bought for us and to see us walk into all we were designed for in full power. Join me as we walk into the fullness of Jesus's Resurrection.

CHAPTER 1

Letting Him Roar

His Roar

To experience the fullness of Jesus, you have to allow Him to show you His power. When you let the Father roar in your life, you are surrendering to Him to let Him show you His power in your life. It is saying to God, "I let you show me your power in this area of my life." When you do this, He will show up in power, and you will experience what He has provided and bought for you! This roar the Father breathes will captivate your life and infuse each area, transforming it into all that He designed for you and desired for you to have!

This roar is gentle and kind. I've had times when I've wanted to talk to God about an issue I'm having or a bad conversation I had, but I was afraid to talk to Him and hear what He wanted to say because I was convinced He was going to be upset and tell me I did terribly. But that thought is a lie. Every time I've pushed through that lie and opened my heart to hear Him, He has been gentle, kind, encouraging, and comforting. This is what His roar is like: gentle, kind, powerful, and life-giving—and volatile to the enemy.

The enemy flees at His roar! When you let the Lord roar and show you His power, there is no place for the enemy's false intimidations. In this place of focus on the Father's power, the enemy is belittled and put out of mind. Your focus is on looking into the face of the Father and focusing on what He has said, what He is capable of, and what He has made available for you. And then . . . everything He has for you will be added to you (Matt. 6:33). In this focus on the Father, the power of the enemy is taken, and the enemy's schemes and attempts at illusions and lies disappear. You enter into a flint-like focus (Isa. 50:7) on Jesus and live in the reality of heaven, as everything of the Spirit is revealed and discovered and lived. You are anointed with the oil of the outpouring of the Father, Jesus, and the Holy Spirit. The enemy loses all bearing, and you become slippery to him. You start living in the only reality we were meant to live in: the Father's reality.

When you live in this type of deep relationship with the Father, your whole body, spirit, and soul are changed. You begin to see and think in the Father's reality, and it becomes your only reality. You are so familiar with the way the Holy Spirit thinks that the enemy's arrows bounce off you. When you give the Father the allowance to work His power in your life, everything that is from Him is filtered in, and everything that is not from Him is filtered out. You see Him clearly and know with a heavenly knowledge what His truth over you is. To you, letting Him roar is a place of protection, comfort, and security.

Abounding in Glory

One of the first steps in coming to a place where you can say, "I let you roar" to God is coming into the belief that the Lord is good and that Jesus's Resurrection accomplished more than just freeing us from sin and death. The Father's design and intention for your life are filled with good. He does not make plans for you that would harm you, and He does not bring sickness into your life. This would be inconsistent with His nature. In 2 Corinthians 3:9 (NASB), we get a picture of what is available to us because we have passed through the Resurrection of Jesus: **"For if the ministry of condemnation has glory, much more does the ministry of righteousness abound in glory."** This verse describes a stark difference between how the people before Jesus's Resurrection lived versus how we can live now that His Resurrection has happened. This difference was described as "abounding in glory." This thing called glory is something that the Christian life is supposed to abound in, and it is supposed to be excessive. Several verses later, 2 Corinthians 3:18 (NASB) reads, **"But we all with unveiled face, beholding as in a mirror the glory of the Lord, are being transformed into the same image from glory to glory, just as from the Lord, the spirit."** Verse 18 shows us that this incredible glory is meant to be an ongoing transformation! We are walking a path of discovering and learning more about this glory as we are being transformed by this glory. This wonderful transformation goes on and on until we look so much like the Father that we are inseparable.

So how are we transformed by this glory? What is a life filled with glory supposed to look like? The word *glory* is defined as pride, pleasure, magnificence, great beauty, honor, and renown. Our lives are meant to look like these things because of Jesus's Resurrection. Our lives are meant to be filled with magnificence, beauty, pleasure, and more. This is the end result. As we are being transformed into glory, we experience these things in our lives. We know the ending; we know the "hope," as Paul states in 2 Corinthians 3:12 (NASB): **"Therefore, having such a hope . . . "** The beginning place in which we start this transformation from glory to glory is in our mind, opinions, thoughts, and judgments.[1] Philippians 4:8 (NKJV) tells us to think on things that are considered true, noble, just, pure, lovely, of good report, of virtue, and praiseworthy. The verse reads:

> **Finally, brethren, whatever things are true, whatever things *are* noble, whatever things *are* just, whatever things *are* pure, whatever things *are* lovely, whatever things *are* of good report, if *there is* any virtue and if *there is* anything praiseworthy—meditate on these things.**

This is along the same lines as what glory means in the Greek. The Greek word for glory, *dóxa*, is rooted in the verb *dokéo*,[2] which specifically refers to our thought life: our mind, opinions, thoughts, and judgments.[3] The way you think will affect your ability to experience this glory. There are thought patterns of this world, rooted in a carnal perception of our lives that we have absorbed. These worldly, carnal thought patterns were not the way God intended us to perceive the world, nor were they to influence how we live. These worldly thought patterns bring us back to a carnal mindset that takes us out of the realm of heaven. We aren't meant to live tied to the way a sinful and corrupt world thinks. We are meant to think like Jesus and experience the immeasurable riches of His grace (Eph. 2:7)! Our thought patterns are meant to be from God, Jesus, and the Holy Spirit and be magnificent, beautiful, and pleasing, full of honor, renown, and pride.

To experience the fullness of Christ, we first begin by starting the process of letting Jesus transform our minds (Rom. 12:2 NIV), thoughts, and thought patterns to look like and think like Jesus:

> **Do not conform to the pattern of this world, but be transformed by the renewing of your mind. Then you will be able to test and approve what God's will is—his good, pleasing and perfect will.**

We are then called to discover all that the Father, Jesus, and Holy Spirit have for us! Ephesians 2:6–7 says:

> **And [God] raised us up with him [Jesus] and seated us with him in the heavenly places in Christ Jesus, so that in the coming ages he might show the immeasurable riches of his grace in kindness toward us in Christ Jesus.**

We are seated with Jesus in heaven, and in this place, God wants to show us the immeasurable riches of His grace! This verse is saying that when we as Christians were born again, God intentionally sat us in heaven with Jesus so that He could show us all the amazing and glorious things that Jesus bought for us for *while we are still on earth.* And 1 Corinthians 2:12 (NASB) says, **"Now we have received, not the spirit of the world, but the Spirit who is from God, so that we may know the things freely given to us by God."** Jesus made so many things available to us through His Resurrection, and through the Holy Spirit, we are called to discover these things freely given to us! God so designed for us to live in such a fullness of His grace, His riches, His Spirit, Jesus's Resurrection, and His reality that He couldn't wait till we got to heaven to share it with us. He had to give it to us now, while we were still on earth. And He invites us to discover and to let Him show us everything that He ever designed for us, right now.

Dóxa (or glory) in its verb form, *dokéo*, also means to suppose,[4] as in to think about, hypothesize, or discover. Our lives are meant to be rich in discovery, overflowing every day with new things from the Spirit that Jesus has made available to us because of His Resurrection and our reunification with God's reality. We are invited to move out of the way this world thinks and move into the way Jesus, the Father, and the Holy Spirit think so that we can experience every good thing Jesus bought for us on the cross.

When we allow this transformation, things start to look different. In 2 Corinthians 4:10 (NASB), it says, **"Always carrying about in the body the dying of Jesus, so that *the life of Jesus also may be manifested in our body*"** (italics mine). There is meant to be a physical marker and distinction as we are being transformed by this glory. Not only our minds but our appearances as well are meant to be filled with magnificence, beauty, pleasure, honor, renown, and pride. Our spirits, minds, and bodies are meant to be transformed as we live in the fullness of Jesus's Resurrection.

There is an ongoing transformation every day as we interact with Holy Spirit, as He shows us new dimensions of what we have access to. Our lives are meant to experience this glory and this transformation abundantly, and as 2 Corinthians 3:9 would put it, we are meant to **"abound in glory."**

Abundant in the Greek means excessive, vehement, advantageous—all-around excess, exceeding expectation![5] This definition shows us the insane measure to which we can live out this transformation of our mind, thoughts, and body and discover all that Jesus, God, and the Holy Spirit want to show and teach us.

CHAPTER 2

Heaven on Earth

Freedom from the Law of Sin and Death

When we are saved, we come out of the law of sin and death and come under the law of the Spirit of life. Romans 8:2 (NASB) says, **"For the law of the Spirit of life in Christ Jesus has set you free from the law of sin and of death."** We have come out from the way the law of sin and death functions and are now under the law of the Spirit of life and live in its ways! We don't have to play by the rules of sin and death anymore. They don't apply to us anymore. We are freed from those rules.

One day our stovetop controls had broken, and we could no longer turn off the burners, which meant we had to turn the stove on and off at the breaker box. A little while later, our new stovetop came with controls that worked. After that new stovetop was installed, I no longer needed to flip the breaker when I wanted to use the stovetop. It took a couple of days to get used to this change, but imagine if I never adjusted my rhythms and still constantly turned the breaker on and off when I used the new stovetop, despite having gotten a new stovetop with controls that worked? It is the same way when we came out from under the law of sin and death and came under the law of the Spirit of life. We are freed from everything that the law of sin and death entails and get to function in Jesus's freedom. We no longer need to function like we are still under the law of sin and death. We now live under the freedoms Jesus gave us.

Anything that falls under the old law of sin and death, we have the heavenly right to not receive. Jesus paid the price for our sin and freed us from having to pay that price. By freeing us from sin and death, Jesus also set us free from *every other* rule of the law of sin and death. We are invited by Jesus Himself to stop living under the functions and norms of sin and death and live in His heavenly reality. Instead of being forced to live a life according to sin and death, Jesus bought our freedom and then invited us to live in all the fullness of His original design for us.

His Kingdom

Matthew 6:10 says, **"Your kingdom come, your will be done, on earth as it is in heaven."** Jesus brought us out of the law of sin and death and into His law of the Spirit of life and the kingdom of heaven. This verse is part of a larger portion of scripture known as the Lord's Prayer. This prayer is the way Jesus showed us to posture our hearts and minds toward God and our expectations of Him, orienting our minds and expectations to experience God's kingdom and to have earth look like heaven. The way heaven functions is the way we are meant to function. We are meant to experience God's kingdom right now and experience all the goodness of heaven right now.

Luke 17:21 is another verse that shows us that we have access to the kingdom of God right now: **"Nor will they say, 'Look, here it is!' or 'There!' for behold, the kingdom of God is in the midst of you."** The kingdom of God is in our midst. The kingdom of God and all of heaven is available for us to live in now. It is in this revelation of what we can live in right now that Jesus said in the Lord's Prayer that we are to posture our hearts and minds toward living as it is in heaven. When we are saved, a heaven-on-earth life is what Jesus bought for us. The characteristics of heaven should be our reality. We are meant to experience the realities of heaven in our daily lives. All the good things that are part of heaven are meant for us right now. Jesus's Resurrection gives us access to heaven and to all the good things God originally designed for us to experience and live in.

In 2 Corinthians 5:17 it says, **"Therefore, if anyone is in Christ, he is a new creation. The old has passed away; behold, the new has come."** The old things of sin and death have passed away and do not apply to us anymore. They are incompatible with who we are in Jesus. We are completely new, and we have been completely separated from the ways, the functions, and the realities of sin and death. We are free!

Because we have been set free from the things of sin and death and can live in the realities of heaven, we can say no to anything that is part of the law of sin and death or that wouldn't be in heaven.

At the time God first showed me this idea of fully living in a heavenly reality, I didn't wear earrings very much. I absolutely loved wearing earrings, but I couldn't . . . because every time I wore earrings, my piercings would have an allergic reaction to the metals in the earrings, turn red and sore, and take days to heal. But then I had the thought, "Allergies are totally caused by sin and death and absolutely won't be a thing in heaven." So I stopped, and I rebuked the authority of the allergies over my ear piercings. I commanded my ears to come into alignment with Jesus's Resurrection and the way God originally created my ears to function. The next time I wore earrings, my piercings worked perfectly and have continued to function well. There have been a few times where the allergy has tried to return, but in those moments I rebuke its authority to be there and *do not* receive back the allergy. Now when I wear earrings, no matter the kind of metal in the earrings or how long I wear them, my ears react perfectly, and they don't get sore or turn red.

This is what we have been invited into when Jesus set us free from sin and death and invited us to live under the law of the Spirit of life and to experience all that we would in heaven. So now when I encounter things like this, I ask myself, "Is there any [blank] in heaven? Is this a thing caused by sin and death?" If it is, then I have the absolute right to rebuke it and claim my right to proper alignment with Jesus's Resurrection, heaven, and how God originally designed me to function.

After being healed of my earring allergy, I began to try out this freedom given to me by Jesus's Resurrection with other things—most notably at the time, my hair. I liked to let my hair air dry. But when I did, it usually got frizzy and didn't look nice.

So I thought to myself, "Will there be frizzy and difficult hair in heaven?" And the answer to that was no. My hair will function perfectly in heaven. While I was having these thoughts, I passed a mirror. There was also a mirror on the opposing wall. Basically, every time I walked through that doorway, there was a mirror to see myself in. While walking, I rebuked my frizz and my hair's dysfunction and commanded my hair to function like it would in heaven and to become smooth, soft, and shiny. I walked back through the doorway and saw no noticeable change in my hair. A few minutes later, I walked through the doorway again. This time my hair looked different. It had lost some of its frizz. It felt like the coolest thing ever. Later that night after dinner, I was getting ready for bed in my bathroom. I sat in front of the mirror and could tell that my hair was frizzy again. So I rebuked the frizz again and commanded my hair to function properly again. Right there in the mirror, I watched the front portion of my hair physically change shape by losing its frizz and becoming soft and shiny. This blew my mind and made me so excited!

God designed for us to live a life that is not subjugated to the norms of sin and death. Instead, He reunited us with everything good. Paul tells us in 2 Corinthians 4:10 (NASB) that life can be manifested in our bodies because of Jesus's Resurrection: **"Always carrying about in the body the dying of Jesus, so that *the life of Jesus also may be manifested in our body*"** (italics mine). Paul is reminding us that our bodies are meant to be full of life and healing. We have a claim to have Jesus's Resurrection power manifest in our bodies and bring alignment and healing to our bodies. We see in 1 Corinthians 2:12 (NASB): **"Now we have received, not the spirit of the world, but the Spirit who is from**

God, so that we may know the things freely given to us by God." God invites us to interact with the Holy Spirit and uncover the treasures He has freely given to us. God wants us to live a life as it would be in heaven. He wants us to discover His goodness and all the things Jesus bought for us on the cross. His desire is for us to be whole and for us to live in that wholeness. Ephesians 2:7 (NASB) says, **"So that in the ages to come He might show the surpassing [incomparable] riches of His grace in kindness toward us in Christ Jesus."** The Greek word here for grace, *cháris*, means kindness, but it also means "to share benefit."[1] So this verse could also read, "So that in the ages to come He might show the surpassing riches of His benefits, in kindness toward us in Christ Jesus." God wants us to experience all His benefits! God separated us from the laws and rules of sin and death and turned the tables so that we could live in all His goodness, all His benefits, all of heaven, and all His healing. This is the life we are invited to live when we are saved. Jesus's Resurrection is the fullness of life.

CHAPTER 3

Thoughts, the Enemy, and the Garden of Eden

The Enemy and His Persuasion

We have been freed from the law of sin and death and have entered the law of the Spirit of Life, but the enemy is at work trying to persuade us that we are still under the law of sin and death. The enemy feeds us lies that seem persuasive, realistic, and plausible, but these lies play by the rules of sin and death. We yield our wonderful freedoms and gifts that come from the Spirit of life when we are persuaded to believe these lies of the enemy. These lies suppress the truth that we are free from every aspect of the law of sin and death and the truth that we can fully live under the law of the Spirit of life.

In 1 Peter 5:8 (NKJV) it says, **"Be sober, be vigilant; because your adversary the devil walks about like a roaring lion, seeking whom he may devour."** This verse shows us that the devil is trying to oppose us by devouring us, but this verse also posits the idea that the devil can't do this alone. The word "may" here is a conditional word and a word that means he needs permission—an inroad. This word is not an absolute.

"Devour" means to consume both *body* and soul. The verse is saying that the devil needs an opportunity to consume your body. The devil does not have absolute power, and this verse shows us that He does not even have the power to consume your body. The enemy needs a second piece. He needs you to be off your guard and oblivious to what is yours in Christ to be able to attack your body. The enemy can only come to us with lies. That is his only power. It's when we are persuaded and believe these lies that we give the enemy the opportunity for him to spring his trap. When this happens we yield our freedoms to the enemy, giving him the right to bring sickness, pains, discomfort, and misalignment in our bodies. But our new reality in Christ is that we have been freed from everything that comes with the law of sin and death. We have the heavenly right to reject anything that comes from the law of sin and death.

The enemy comes and tells us lies, but he also comes armed with persuasion and the validation of the problem. He tells the lie and then tries to present evidence that supports it. The enemy brings persuasion and validation to his lies. These lies often come in the form of worldly thought patterns, thought patterns that play by the rules of sin and death. One of these thought patterns might be, "Of course my kid got sick. He went to that birthday party last week with all those other kids." The sickness or cold is something that is part of the law of sin and death, which we have the right to reject. But the enemy, coming with lies and persuasion, brings his validation of the sickness by giving you the validating thought that your kid got sick from the party. The enemy's lie here is that *cause and effect* cannot be denied. This lying thought pattern from the enemy says that since there is an obvious reason as to why you are suffering this, you must receive it. The truth is that the cold your kid got from the birthday party can be fully rejected and commanded to leave, because Jesus, on the cross, freed us from sickness and anything else that would fall under the law of sin and death. Sickness does not have authority over you anymore.

Some of the other thought patterns that follow the "cause and effect" persuasion are the simple conclusions we form that make us feel like we have to just deal with it, but here is the truth: "Even if there is a lot of pollen in the air, I can rebuke congestion and allergies and expect them to leave"; "Even though I ran into that door frame, I can still rebuke a bruise from forming and any other side effects like aches or pains"; "Even though flu season is coming, I refuse to partner with the expectation that I will inevitably get sick, because the flu is incompatible with my body since it is under the law of the Spirit of life." These are some examples of the truth and of the fullness of Christ that we can live in.

Colossians 2:8–9 warns us against listening to and believing these lies of the enemy that are masked as human reasoning:

> **See to it that no one takes you captive by philosophy and empty deceit, according to human tradition, according to the elemental spirits of the world, and not according to Christ. For in him the whole fullness of deity dwells bodily.**

The Passion Translation also offers helpful insight into what this verse means:

> **Beware that no one distracts you or intimidates you** *in their attempt to lead you away from Christ's fullness* **by pretending to be full of wisdom when they're filled with endless arguments of human logic. For they operate with humanistic and clouded judgments based on the mindset of this world system, and not the anointed truths of the Anointed One. For he is the complete fullness of deity living in human form.**

The way this world thinks and reasons is inspired by sin and the enemy and is not how we are meant to reason. We are invited by Christ to live in His spiritual realm, where we are free from the ways and the logic of the world and can live in His fullness.

When we live in the anointed truths of Jesus and the truth that we are completely free from the ways of this world, sin, and death, we get to live in all the fullness of Christ. When we choose to turn a blind eye to the lies of the enemy and decide to live in the truths of Jesus and His freedom, we void the enemy of any power. It's when we entertain the enemy's lies and accept the sickness, pains, misalignment, etcetera that we give those lies and those problems power over us. We are free. These sicknesses, pains, and anything that would be misaligned in our bodies are the realities of this world, but they are not our reality in Christ. We are in this world, but we are foreigners here (1 Pet. 2:11); the things of this world are foreign to us. They are so incompatible with us and our new creation in Christ that the enemy must exhaust all his resources to try to persuade and convince us that we are compatible with these things and that we have no other option than to live with them.

That lie comes from a victim spirit and is the opposite of Jesus's Spirit of power, described in 2 Timothy 1:7: **"For God gave us a spirit not of fear but of power and love and self-control."** Jesus's spirit gives us power. It does not subjugate us to this world. We are called to be free in Jesus's realm and reality. We are meant to live free from every thought and pattern of this world.

The Garden of Eden

Jesus reversed everything that happened in the Garden of Eden. In the Garden of Eden, the law of sin and death entered and took authority over the world. God in that moment, with Adam and Eve, mentioned some of the effects of sin entering the world:

> **[To the serpent he said] "I will put enmity between you and the woman, and between your offspring and her offspring; he shall bruise your head, and you shall bruise his heel." To the woman he said, "I will surely multiply your pain in childbearing; in pain you shall bring forth children. Your desire shall be contrary to your husband, but he shall rule over you." And to Adam he said, "Because you have listened to the voice of your wife and have eaten of the tree**

of which I commanded you, 'You shall not eat of it,' cursed is the ground because of you; in pain you shall eat of it all the days of your life; thorns and thistles it shall bring forth for you; and you shall eat the plants of the field. By the sweat of your face you shall eat bread, till you return to the ground, for out of it you were taken; for you are dust, and to dust you shall return." (Gen. 3:15–19)

One thing that is important to note is that this list of things mentioned are effects of sin and death. They are not punishments from God. God does not bring pain, sickness, or death; it goes against God's nature to bring such things. Our God is a God of mercy, goodness, kindness, healing, gentleness, and grace. God, here, identifies that sin has entered the world and explains some of the key areas affected and tainted by sin and death: pregnancy complications, birthing pains, male dominance, weeds, deterioration in old age, and mortality. Family strife also became a part of Adam's and Eve's lives after sin and death entered the world.

In the first two-thirds of verse 16, we are shown that pregnancy complications and birthing pains are effects of sin and death. The first half of this thought in verse 16 reads, **"I will surely multiply your pain in *childbearing*"** (italics mine). This refers to the process of bearing the child, the nine-month journey of carrying the baby. The second half of this thought reads, **"In pain you shall bring forth children."** This is referring to the actual process of birthing the baby, or labor. This verse is showing us that both pregnancy complications and labor pains are effects of sin and death.

The rest of verse 16 explains to us that husbands will rule over their wives, an effect of sin and death that says men will believe that women are inferior to them. Male dominance was not something that God originally designed. It is a thought that comes from the law of sin and death.

Verses 17 and 18 explain to us that because of sin and death, the ground will now bear weeds. Finally, in verse 19, we are shown that bodily deterioration and mortality are also effects of sin and death; it says that we will continue working on the earth until we return to the ground. This shows us a picture of our bodies wearing out and eventually fully manifesting in mortal death.

In this moment in the garden, God explained what was going to happen to the world because the law of sin and death was now in power, but amid this, we are also shown the ending point. In verse 15, we see a prophecy of Jesus coming and defeating Satan: **"He [Jesus] shall bruise your head, and you shall bruise his heel."** This prophecy was given as an ending point for sin and death. It is the point when the serpent or Satan is defeated. This verse does not say that the ending point is when we get to heaven or when we get to the new earth. It is right now. Jesus has come, and we can be separated from all the power of sin, from all the power of death, from all the power of the things mentioned in the garden, and from all the power of Satan. Jesus on the cross reversed everything. He freed us from everything that was a result of sin and death. We are free from pregnancy complications; we are free from pain in childbirth; we are free from strife in our families. The thoughts that make us refrain from receiving these truths are the lies of the enemy that say, "This is the world we live in. We have to receive the things that come from sin and death"; "Birthing pains are normal. I have to receive them"; "There is a plausible reason as to why I have this pregnancy complication. I have to receive it."

Jesus revoked the rights of those things over our lives. Jesus reversed everything that happened in the garden and set us free from playing by the rules of sin and death. The enemy tries to come and tell us that we are still under the things of sin and death and that we must receive them, but we have the heavenly right to say no and reject them: to reject and rebuke pregnancy complications or pain in childbirth, and to command our gardens to receive the reconciliation and peace that Jesus bought and to stop bearing weeds. Our reality is the realm of Heaven with Jesus.

It is easy to reject and receive healing from these things when they get out of hand, such as "My pregnancy complication is restricting airflow to my baby." In that moment, people usually ask God for healing and hopefully expect that healing for their problem. But we tend to receive the problems when they are tolerable, seem normal, or are on a lesser scale, such as "I have itchy skin from my pregnancy" or "My back hurts all the time during my third trimester." We have a right to reject these things too. We are freed from every little thing of sin and death.

Another one of the things mentioned in the garden of Eden was deterioration in old age. We can see this in Genesis 3:19 when it says that we will eventually, over time, turn back to dust: "**By the sweat of your face you shall eat bread, till you return to the ground, for out of it you were taken; for you are dust, and to dust you shall return.**" Our freedom in Christ also includes freedom from our bodies deteriorating in old age and because of wear and tear. This is God's design for you: to be completely whole in your body; for your body to never wear out; and to never function less than how God originally designed your body.

God wrote this into our salvation in **John 3:16**. It reads, **"For God so loved the world, that he gave his only Son, that whoever believes in him should not perish but have eternal life."** We typically take this verse to mean eternal life in heaven. This is true, but the word for eternal life here refers to both our life in heaven *and* to our life while we are on earth.[1] This verse is saying that we should not perish while we are here on earth but instead have life. To *perish* means to waste away and decay. So in its entirety, this verse can be read, "That whoever believes in him should not waste away and decay but have fullness of life right now and in the future."

Jesus said that He wants to give us full, abundant life (John 10:10). His design for us is to no longer live under the effects and rules of sin and death. This includes freedom from having our bodies deteriorate as we live and use them, as well as in old age. This includes freedom from every result of getting old, including sicknesses like Alzheimer's, memory loss, and muscle deterioration.

Jesus reversed everything that sin, death, and Satan did, and His ways are the opposite of the enemy's ways. John 10:10 reads, **"The thief comes only to steal, kill, and destroy. I came that they may have life and have it abundantly."** The NLT translation would read the second half of this verse as, **"My [Jesus's] purpose is to give them a rich and satisfying life."** Jesus reversed everything the enemy did. Jesus is the opposite of sickness, pain, death, and any other thing that would come against our bodies. Jesus is healing, and His desire for us is to live abundantly in healing and the fullness of life. Jesus wants you to have life in your body. Living under sickness, pains, and the wasting away of our bodies is not life. Jesus is the opposite of these things, and He brings wholeness with Him; he came to reverse everything the enemy did and everything that happened in the Garden of Eden. Because of this, we get to share in every good thing and benefit that Jesus, the Father, and the Holy Spirit have for us. This is Jesus's design for us: to live in His fullness of life right now as we reject the things of the enemy and reject the things of sin and death.

No Longer Bound by the Carnal Realm

The effects of sin and death are part of our carnal realm and our carnal perception, which is the physical world around us that we perceive with our eyes. But these effects of sin and death are not in effect in the kingdom of heaven. Jesus's heavenly realm became our only true reality when we were saved. But the enemy tries to persuade us into thinking that this carnal realm is still our reality. Things like deteriorating as we age do not have to be our reality, but when we listen to the plausible persuasion of the enemy, deterioration becomes our perceived reality. We do not have to accept the things of this carnal realm's reality. The effects of sin and death do not have authority over us anymore unless we give them authority. But you have the authority to rebuke and reject these effects of sin and death.

I rebuked wear and tear in my body once when I was mopping my dining room. The floor was extra muddy and dirty and difficult to clean. I was mopping hard, rigorously going back and forth on the same area multiple times, and could feel the muscles in my arms were getting very tired. I thought to myself, "I need to take a break!" But then I realized that exhaustion and wear of my muscles was a thing of sin and death and was not how God intended my body to function. So I rebuked the exhaustion and the wear on my muscles and declared over my muscles to have full strength and to function properly. I continued to mop, and my muscles had regained full strength. I finished mopping without another thought about my arms, because there was no exhaustion after that.

We have received a spirit of power from our Father and have a right to receive all His life right now. The things we consider normal, like having allergies in the spring or having arthritis in old age, are not inspired by our Father and are not our own thoughts either. They are the persuasion of the enemy, who tries to convince us that we must live with the dysfunction created by sin and death. But in reality, we are completely free from all these effects and can live in full freedom from them in Christ. We are called to see and think in the heavenly realm, not the carnal realm that is polluted with sin, death, dysfunction, sickness, and misalignment. Those things are no longer compatible with us since we were made new in Christ. Jesus invites us to step out of this familiar carnal realm and into His heavenly realm. He has given us an invitation to total freedom and life untainted by this realm.

These carnal things only have power over us when we are convinced they do. If we believe we are subject to any and every cold that goes around, then that cold will have authority over us. But when we instead choose to believe the truth and freedom of Jesus, we break the lie that says we have no choice but to be subject to the things of this world and the effects of sin and death. It is in this truth that sin, death, and Satan lose their power, and we come into the freedom Jesus bought for us.

Our Freedom in Christ

Romans 8:1–2 (NASB) says, **"Therefore there is now no condemnation for those who are in Christ Jesus. For the law of the Spirit of life in Christ Jesus has set you free from the law of sin and of death."** We are not meant to be condemned to the law of sin and death, its effects, and its norms. Through His Resurrection, Jesus voided all these effects in our lives. We no longer have to live a life where we feel condemned to the ways that sin and death, sickness, allergies, chaos, family strife, pain, deterioration, and wear and tear function. We are not condemned. We are free and have been given the heavenly power of Jesus.

In chapter 1, we explored 2 Corinthians 3:9, which showed us that our Christian lives are meant to be filled with glory, or *dóxa*[2] in the Greek. This word means "praise, honor, divine glory, splendor"[4] and "the unspoken manifestation of God."[5] Our lives are meant to look like those words. The things of our lives are meant to be praiseworthy; sickness and deterioration are not praiseworthy. Our lives are meant to be filled with honor; honor is health and wholeness in every area of our lives—in our interactions with family members and also in our bodies. Our lives are meant to be full of all the divine glory of God and His unspoken manifestation, which is discovering new dimensions of His freedom. Our lives are meant to be full of splendor; this is excellence and blessing from the Father in every area of our lives. This is the Father's design for our lives.

God's design and desire for us would be for us to function in this freedom. Jesus has already bought this freedom for us, but we also must choose to receive it. Jesus gave us authority over the enemy, sin, and death, but it is still up to us whether we receive the authority Jesus gave us or yield our heavenly power and begin to receive the things of this world.

We are meant to walk in Scripture with conviction. We are meant to believe what it says and to live in it. God has given us freedom and the truth that we are completely free from the law of sin and of death and all its effects. His desire is that we would believe this truth and walk in it with complete conviction. He desires for us to walk in this heavenly power He has given us and to reject the things of this carnal world.

We are meant to experience Jesus's power constantly in our lives each moment. His power is meant to be evident in our lives in every area. Our God is a God of power. We are not meant to go a moment without experiencing His wonderful power. God's design for every Christian is for them to live in freedom and in His power. We have a wonderful God of power, who has given us everything that is His in Jesus's Resurrection. We have a heavenly right to function in Jesus's power and have been called to live in it and experience it.

CHAPTER 4

Stepping Stones

Rebuke and Receive

Jesus has given us these truths that we learned about in chapter 3 that we are free from every effect of sin and death and that He has given us many freedoms for us to live in and to see manifested in our lives. When Jesus gave us these truths, He also gave us the power to walk them out in our lives. In 1 Corinthians 2:12–13 (NASB), we are shown a picture of how we can walk this out day to day:

> **Now we have received, not the spirit of the world, but the Spirit who is from God, so that we may know the things freely given to us by God, which things we also speak, not in words taught by human wisdom, but in those taught**

by the Spirit, combining spiritual *thoughts* with spiritual *words*.

The first part of this passage establishes that because we have the Holy Spirit, we can now discover the things freely given to us by God and discover all His wonderful benefits and freedoms. God designed for us to continually discover all the wonderful things He has gifted to us. We discover the things freely given to us through reading Scripture and meditating on it, but we also discover these things through the Spirit of God revealing them to us throughout our day. As we interact with the Spirit of God, we can discover new dimensions of His freedom that we never imagined. This freedom is our birthright as children of God, and God desires for us to discover all He has given us.

The second part of this passage in verse 13 tells us what to do with our new revelations of freedom. It tells us to take these things that we've discovered by the Spirit, to take these spiritual thoughts and ideas and declare them out loud. We are meant to declare Jesus's freedoms over ourselves, our bodies, and our families.

We learned in chapters 1 and 3 that glory or *dóxa*[1] means "pride, pleasure, magnificence, great beauty, honor, renown, splendor, and praise,"[2] and that these things are meant to abound in our lives. We've explored a few of the ways glory interacts with and impacts our lives, but there is another facet of this word, dóxa, that shows us how we can experience this complete freedom in our lives. Dóxa is the root of *dogma*,[3] which means "a decree or ordinance."[4] Let's look at the first part of that definition of dogma: decreeing. Along with this pride, pleasure, magnificence, great beauty, honor, renown, splendor, and praise that is meant to be a part of our lives is the invitation to believe and then decree those things into our lives. It is an important part of experiencing this glory in our lives to decree it in and over our lives. This is how I can fully experience His benefits and His glory in my life: when I speak them out loud, confident in the belief that they are mine and standing firm in the belief that the problem I am declaring this glory over *does not* have authority over me.

We are meant to declare this glory into and over our lives. We have become heirs to wonderful freedoms and benefits, but the other half is receiving and invoking these freedoms. When we invoke our freedoms, it is necessary to reject the old things and receive the new things. Rejecting or rebuking the problem doesn't necessarily happen the same way for each problem. When you encounter pain, for example, we know it is not a thing from God and is inspired by sin and death, so it can be rebuked. After rebuking the pain, you then replace it with the thing God has made available to you in place of the pain, such as healing, strength, right alignment, or any other freedom that is opposite of the pain.

But at other times, the thing that you are struggling with is not innately from sin, death, or Satan but has instead been tainted by sin, death, and Satan. The first time God taught this to me, I had recognized that the plaque on my teeth was not good and had negative effects. So I thought I would try to rebuke the plaque. I rebuked the plaque, but I felt the Spirit nudge me that something was off in that statement. What the Holy Spirit told me in that moment was to rebuke the dysfunction of the plaque, not the plaque itself. Plaque was something that sin and death had tainted, something that God originally had designed for a good purpose. The plaque was not the problem; it was the dysfunction created by sin and death that was the problem. After I rebuked the dysfunction of the plaque and the formation of cavities, I then replaced them with the freedom Jesus had for me instead. I declared over my teeth that they would function and interact properly, not develop cavities, and be full of life.

The Spirit showed me here that rebuking the dysfunction was the thing that led to freedom. That was the appropriate thing for this issue. But at other times, or for other issues, it is appropriate to rebuke the thing itself or to revoke the right of the issue. When I run into a new issue and want to declare the freedoms I have in Jesus, I stop and listen to the Spirit to hear how He would attack the issue. For example, one time I had noticed that my bug bites were itching, but as I started to rebuke them, I paused and listened to what the Spirit was wanting to lead me to rebuke. He said to revoke the right of the itch, so I did, and the itching stopped. In each moment you rebuke something, pause to listen to the Spirit for strategy. He will speak to you and show you what to do. He will show you what to rebuke and how to rebuke it, and He will lead you into how to attack the problem. Pause as you go to rebuke and let the Spirit speak and lead your thoughts into how to go about this. He has divine strategy ready for you and has the answer to every question.

The second part of the definition of dogma is an ordinance, which is a law. This glory we are meant to experience is described as a law, fitting with the idea that we are now under the law of the Spirit of life, which is full of this glory. All of our wonderful freedoms and inheritances from our heavenly Father that we've talked about over the last four chapters are permanent laws in our new law of the Spirit of life, given to us through Jesus's Resurrection. This new law we are under (which we explored some in chapter 2) is full of grace and freedom. Every one of our freedoms we've learned about that we have a right to as heirs in Christ have heavenly power and cannot be defeated. Our right to healing and strength throughout our whole lives is final and permanent. These rights and freedoms are ordinances in the new Resurrection life we have in Jesus. They are meant to be part of our walk with Jesus. This healing, strength, and more is cemented as part of our new life in Christ. But we need to believe that we have received these freedoms.

Doubt Is a Lie

What becomes difficult in this moment of receiving these freedoms is when a spirit of fear and doubt comes to persuade us out of the blessings, promises, and freedom that have been given to us. But we know that when the enemy comes, all that he says are lies. His persuasion is a lie. God has given us truth, clarity, and freedom. It is in this moment of realizing the freedom given to us that we should believe the words wholeheartedly, believing that Jesus has already given us the freedom and that all we have to do is receive it. God's words are final. The enemy has no power to change the words God has spoken, but he does seek to stop us from receiving the things spoken by God by causing us to doubt. The enemy wants to stop you from receiving all these things that the Father has for you through inspiring doubt. We get to choose in that moment of doubt to either believe the lie that is doubt or to break through the fog doubt tries to create and believe the words of the Father. Matthew 21:21–22 (NASB) says:

> **And Jesus answered and said to them, "Truly I say to you, if you have faith and do not doubt, you will not only do what was done to the fig tree, but even if you say to this mountain, 'Be taken up and cast into the sea,' it will happen. And all things you ask in prayer, believing, you will receive.**

When we doubt the ability of a word God spoke to actually happen, we stop ourselves from receiving that blessing or freedom. Remember from chapter 1 that experiencing glory starts in our mind and thoughts. Focusing on the certainty of Jesus's words, power, blessing, and freedom He's given us allows us to believe them with a childlike faith that doesn't look around at all the doubt that circumstances, others, or the enemy bring. When you simply believe that the Father's promises and freedoms are real and effective, they will become real and a part of your life in abundance.

James 1:22–24 encourages us to live out the freedoms that are revealed to us in scripture and to not just passively read them over without effect on our lives:

> **But be doers of the word, and not hearers only, deceiving yourselves. For if anyone is a hearer of the word and not a doer, he is like a man who looks intently at his natural face in a mirror. For**

he looks at himself and goes away and at once forgets what he was like.

The words the Father spoke have far more power than the words of doubt. When we choose to believe what He said with a confidence that is absolute, the power doubt has to hold us back evaporates. Doubt can only regain a hold on us when we choose to play with doubt and its persuasion. A childlike faith focuses on the truth and the freedom, not on the doubt. It focuses on the promise, freedom, and statement. God has given power behind every statement of freedom and blessing in the Bible, and He encourages us to live out that power.

Doubt is a lie the enemy tries to get you to believe. *Doubt is a lie.* It has no more bearing on the situation than if someone told you electricity is fake to make you not use it. It is so freeing when you recognize that all the ploys of the enemy are lies. Anything the enemy comes at you with is in actuality lies, whether it's fear, doubt, or any other of his tactics. The enemy's power dissipates and dissolves when you recognize that it is all a lie.

I experienced this feeling of dissipation and dissolving recently with fear. I was going to film a short live video for the first time in a Facebook group where I introduced myself and explained why I wanted to write this book. I had never done this before and was nervous. I realized I was fearing that I would draw a blank or forget my words. But as soon as I recognized that fear was the only thing making me feel bad, I knew it was a lie. When I realized that what I was feeling was inspired by a lie, all the fear left; it just dissolved and dissipated. It was gone, and I had a clear head.

Doubt is the same way. It only has power when you believe it and lean into it. But as soon as you recognize it as a lie, with no actual bearing on reality, it simply dissipates and dissolves, and you can clearly recognize and believe in God's promises, statements, and power.

At first, you may need to go through this process of recognizing and rejecting doubt multiple times in a moment for a particular issue, but the more you train your mind to be centered on the truth and freedom of God, it will become easier and easier for you to partner with what God has said, rejecting doubt until you rarely need to intentionally think about it. When you recognize that doubt is a lie from the enemy and believe that God's words and statements have definite power, His words become real, possible, and attainable!

It has been such a fun and exciting journey of discovering everything I have freedom from because of Jesus, God, and the Holy Spirit. The journey of discovery starts with recognizing things we could be free from, and after we come out from under the lie of doubt, we unleash the power God has given us behind His Scriptures. One of the things I tried early on was rebuking the rough skin on my arms. I decided to do this because I recognized that the rough skin was not intended in the original design of my body by my Creator and that it would not be a thing in heaven. So I rebuked it. Every time I have rebuked the roughness, my skin has returned to smoothness. God has given me authority over anything that is less than He intended, so the roughness has to fall in line with the freedom Jesus has bought for my body. I would rebuke the dysfunction of the rough skin and instead declare my skin to be smooth, soft, and return to how its Creator originally designed it.

A little later after I experienced this, I was visiting some family in Oklahoma, a very hot state. I was out walking to a farmers market and was noticing how warm I was. I thought to myself, "Overheating will not be a thing of heaven," which meant that I had authority to rebuke it. I rebuked the overheating and commanded my body to regulate its temperature properly. I instantly cooled off and was not too warm anymore. I have experienced this same thing in the grocery store, particularly in the freezer section. From the moment I walked into that store I was colder than usual. My sister and I walked to the back of the store to get something from the freezer section. The freezer door was open, and I was standing next to the cart when I realized that my "being too cold" was the same as the overheating I had experienced at the farmers market. Being too cold was also not a thing I was meant to live under. So I rebuked the coldness and commanded my body to warm properly. I instantly was not cold anymore. My hands no longer struggled to move, and I felt normal. Jesus has given us perfect alignment in our bodies, and all we must do to experience it is to choose to live under the freedoms with an open heart.

One of my favorite times of experiencing this alignment in my body was with my menstrual cramps. Pain only became a thing after sin entered the world in the Garden of Eden, but we are free from all those effects because of the death and Resurrection of Jesus. I recognized that cramps and pain during my cycle did not have to have authority in my body anymore. They only had authority in my body when I accepted the menstrual cramps as normal and reasonable. So I would rebuke the cramps when I felt them, and progressively, over my next few cycles, the cramps decreased until I didn't have any before or during my cycle. The cramps and pain did not have authority over my body anymore. When I decided to claim the freedom Jesus bought for me, the effects of sin and death had to come under His rule.

Continue in Faith

It is important to keep believing, even when we don't see results. We see this in a practical way in our lives, such as when we are learning how to ride a bike. When you were little, you would try to keep the bike upright but fail. But you had confidence that it was possible to learn how to ride a bike, so you tried again and again, and eventually were able to ride a bike. This same concept applies to our journey of discovery with Jesus. We easily understand this concept of trying something but having it not work yet, and then trying again in our daily lives, but we don't always translate this concept into our walk with Jesus. We tend to think that if we pray for something or declare something and don't see a result, that it isn't possible or that God said no. But this is not the case. At the beginning of this journey of discovering all my freedoms in Christ, the Father spoke to me: "Even if it doesn't work, it doesn't mean that it can't work." These words had a huge impact on me when the Father spoke them to me, because He is encouraging us to continue in faith and try again, even if we didn't see a result.

One experience I've had with this concept was when I was rebuking the weeds in my flower garden. Weeds are an effect of sin and death, which means that I have authority over them because of Jesus's Resurrection. I walked out to my garden and rebuked the weeds. When I checked back a couple of days later, the weeds were still there. I rebuked the weeds again but still saw no result. A year later, we moved to a new house with an undeveloped backyard. I tried again rebuking the weeds in my new garden at my new house. The next time I went to look at my garden, the weeds had decreased and significantly gone down. It was as if the weeds just disappeared. The authority and freedoms that Jesus bought for us are absolute. I don't need to fear that they won't work. Jesus gave them to me, and Jesus has the final say. Don't be discouraged if you don't see a result when you rebuke something. Take heart, try again, and have confident faith in the authority that Jesus gave you!

Repetition and Belief

As God was teaching me all these things about Him and His freedom that He has gifted to us, I asked Him the question, "How do I make the thing I rebuked not return and the declaration I made stick?" What He spoke to me in that moment was, "Repetition and the belief that it doesn't have authority over you." Later I asked God what He meant by repetition. What he showed me was that repetition is getting your heart to a place where it believes. I've had times where I go to rebuke something, but I can feel that I don't believe the statement I'm saying. Your power comes from your belief.

In those moments, it is necessary to do something to get your heart to a place where it believes the statement, and God said that repetition can do that. Repetition melds the words of your declaration with your heart and mind and bolsters your spirit to believe the statement that is meant to be your reality. In those moments I like to repeat the words "I believe" several times until I can feel my spirit lifted and my heart encouraged; then, when I say my statement, I can feel the power and authority that comes behind it. I don't do this same thing every time, and God will teach you how to do this repetition specifically for you. The goal is to put belief behind your declaration and to truly believe the words coming out of your mouth. When you believe the words, they have power.

God also spoke to me about "the belief that it doesn't have authority over you." Repetition helps you get to the place where you believe your statement, and then the belief that it doesn't have authority over you propels you forward and sustains the freedom like an anti-enemy-scheme spray. This belief is your mindset. It comes into play first when you rebuke the issue, but it is also the mindset you keep as you walk forward. It is your confidence that Jesus has set you free and that you have authority over the problem. This belief holds you firm if the sickness or pain tries to return. You have authority over the problem, so it is important to not receive again the problem if it tries to come back. Let's say you rebuke your back pain, it leaves, and then tomorrow or a week or a month later, you feel that same pain again. You have a choice in that moment to receive again the pain and accept it or to stand firm in the belief that you have authority over the back pain. In that moment, you stand firm in that belief and tell the pain it doesn't have a right to come back into your body. The pain has already had its authority taken away once; what you are doing here is telling it that it can't have that authority back. When the pain or the problem tries to return, it does not mean that you failed, that you did something wrong, or that God said no to your healing. We want to stand firm in our authority and say no to the return of the problem. God is with you.

No Weight from Responsibility

This freedom we are learning to function in is an inheritance and a gift given to us by our heavenly Father. We are meant to enjoy this inheritance, not feel an obligation from it. I remember one day I was feeling tired and had decided to go take a nap. As I was walking to my room, I heard the Lord say, "Wait, wait, wait," as if He was excited to show me something.

I replied, "Yes?" and paused to listen to Him.

He said to me, "This tiredness can be rebuked too." Those words were so exciting to me and represented a whole new level of freedom available to us to live in. I rebuked the tiredness and commanded my body to be full of rest and life. Instantly, the tiredness left me, and I felt great!

I was so excited at this revelation, but then, in that moment, I felt worried and asked God, "Do I now have to rebuke tiredness every single time I feel tired?"

He instantly replied, "No." He showed me that the freedom Jesus has bought us is freeing and is a light yoke. It is not a weighty, heavy yoke full of rigorous rules to follow. Our Father wants a relationship with us, not to give us a list of rules. This journey of freedom He has invited us on is one of gentleness and relationship.

We are not meant to feel heavy and burdened on this journey but to experience the lightness and delightfulness of the freedom Jesus bought for us through His Resurrection.

The Father told me that this is what childlike faith is like. It does not feel a weight from responsibility. We have been given wonderful freedoms to experience and discover, and the Father's heart is that we would experience these freedoms with full delight and joy like a child, not with a heavy yoke or a feeling of burden. This freedom is light, delightful, pleasant, full of beauty, and gentle. This is how we are meant to feel when we experience this freedom.

We are meant to rely on our heavenly Father. When we stop relying on Him, our fear of doing something wrong, striving, or feeling a weight from responsibility become heavy and weigh us down, but what God said about His glory is that it will be full of pride, pleasure, magnificence, great beauty, honor, renown, praise, and splendor. As we rely on Him, we get to enjoy this freedom without taking on a weight or burden. Our Father has given us something delightful to enjoy as His prized son or daughter.

It's Not a Fight

This delightful freedom He has given us is the final authority and gives us authority. We are not fighting for our freedom. Jesus has already won it. We have been given authority and get to enjoy this freedom He's given to us. This freedom Jesus has given us through His Resurrection is a light yoke and gives us the ability to simply receive and enjoy our freedoms. When we step into a new level of our freedom from sin, death, and the enemy—perhaps by rebuking something or receiving healing—we are not fighting the enemy as if we need to win and steal our freedom from him. The enemy has no power. The only warring we need to do is to choose to receive our freedom by believing that we have been given authority over the issue. You choose to believe that the enemy, sin, and death are not the ruling powers over your life. Our Father is our ruling power, and He protects us and lavishes us with a passion we have never seen before. We are not playing a tug-of-war game with the enemy when we are rebuking something and receiving freedom. We are believing in our authority over the enemy. All we need to do is receive our freedom. It isn't a fight—just a victory field.

Freedom in Atmospheres

We've learned that the effects of sin, death, and the enemy can be rebuked in our bodies, but they can also be rebuked in our atmospheres and the surroundings of our lives. We saw in the Garden of Eden that after sin entered the world, family strife came into existence as well. Family strife is an effect of sin and death that we can rebuke and reject, just as we would rebuke knee pain or hearing loss. I've experienced the effects of a spirit of family strife before and have quietly rebuked it and seen it stop affecting the atmosphere. We see this theme of being able to rebuke and reject negative atmospheres in Romans 8:1: **"There is therefore now no condemnation for those who are in Christ Jesus."** Condemnation is an effect that came from sin and death. Here, this verse is showing us that feelings like condemnation can be rejected and rebuked. They are no longer something that we have to be subjected to. These feelings and atmospheres that do not come from the Lord—like condemnation, family strife, and other negative atmospheres are things we have been freed from.

The authority of sin, death, and the enemy over our lives in every way has been taken away completely by Jesus's Resurrection. When you notice or sense that something is "off" in the atmosphere—for example, if the morning with your family is feeling chaotic, you can rebuke that spirit of chaos and invite Jesus to fill the atmosphere with His peace, or you can ask Jesus what He would like to give you in place of the chaotic environment and invite that. Sin, death, and the enemy don't have authority in our lives anymore, and anything they bring to the table can be rejected. Our lives are meant to be filled with total peace, pride, pleasure, magnificence, great beauty, honor, renown, praise, and splendor. This is the kind of life we have been invited to. Our Father does not want us to live bound up by any of the ways the world functions. He has bought total freedom for us right now!

John 16:33 shows us that Jesus has bought every type of freedom for everything we could encounter. It reads, **"I have said these things to you, that in me you may have peace. In the world you will have tribulation. But take heart; I have overcome the world."** I've always thought this verse was saying that we will have tribulation in this life and that there is no way to escape it. But what this verse highlights is that Jesus overcomes the tribulation, and that He has every solution. The way the world functions is with problems and the effects of sin and death, but how you and I are meant to function as part of Christ is in freedom from those things. We are in Christ now, and He has overcome all the things of the world.

This verse is highlighting that because we are in Christ, we have peace. He has given us freedom from every problem we may encounter and has given us freedom in Him that goes deeper than we could have ever imagined. We are totally free!

CHAPTER 5

Other Areas of Freedom (Part 1)

All Areas Full of Him and Freedom

The wonderful freedom Jesus gave us from sin and death through His Resurrection extends to every area of our lives: our bodies and our atmospheres, but also in places like our finances and wants and desires. When Jesus died on the cross and rose again, He gave us blessings and freedom in every possible area of our lives. Scripture would say that He filled all things with Himself. Jesus is freedom, so He filled every area of our lives with freedom. Jesus is blessing, so He filled every area of our lives with blessing. He is attentive to our lives in each task we do and to our thoughts and desires. Ephesians 1:22–23 says, **"And he put all things under his feet and gave him as head over all things to the church, which is his body, the fullness of him who fills all in all."** The NLT words the end of Ephesians 1:23 as **"who fills all things everywhere with himself."** Our Father is interested in every detail of our lives and cares about all those areas. He wants to interact with you in all you do.

I love to bake and create my own recipes. As I bake, I've discovered that the Father likes to talk to me, giving me advice and ideas. Recently, when I was making a chocolate cake, I was trying to decide how much milk to put in. As I was going to grab the jug of milk, He spoke to me and told me not to add any milk. I was a little shocked at first, because milk is a relatively important ingredient in a cake. But I recognized the voice and the presence that came with the statement and knew it was Him. So I didn't add any milk, and after my cake was baked, I was so glad I hadn't added any. Our Father's desire is to interact with us in all we do, no matter what it is. He cares about what we care about, even if it seems small to us.

Our heavenly Father loves to interact with us. He died on the cross and rose again so that He and the Holy Spirit would be available to us in every moment, in everything, and in every area of our lives, with no area or thing excluded. He doesn't want to be separated from anything we do or anything we experience. He loves us and loves to do life with us!

Ask and Receive

In Matthew 21:22, Jesus gives us this statement: **"And whatever you ask in prayer, you will receive, if you have faith."** We know that our Father's desire is to give us all the riches of His glory, the fullness of heaven, all of His benefits, and that He wants to show us all the things freely given to us by Him. He wants our lives to be full of His glory, which (as we explored earlier) means that He wants our lives to be full of praise, honor, splendor, pride, pleasure, magnificence, great beauty, and renown. Our lives are to be full of continual discovery of the blessings and freedoms He has given to us.

And then Jesus gave us a verse like **Matthew 21:22, "And whatever you ask in prayer, you will receive, if you have faith."** We learned in chapter 3 it is His desire that we would confidently believe the things He said in Scripture, and walk in them with conviction. His desire is that we would believe the words of Matthew 21:22: to believe that He is a Father who loves to bless us exceedingly and abundantly, more than we could ever dream; to believe that He wants to lavish us and make our lives full of good things; and to believe that if we ask Him for something, His answer will be yes.

One of the times I experienced this was regarding my college homework. I was studying full time but had different start dates for all my classes, so at first I only had two classes. During this time, I had been in a rhythm of finishing my work on Monday and Tuesday, but the next week, another two of my classes were going to start. Normally, I would also work all day Wednesday with four classes, but I was enjoying having Wednesday free. I was sitting on my bed when I thought, "But I'm not going to ask God to be able to still finish all my work by Tuesday." That felt like a ridiculous request and in the realm of impossibility.

But as soon as I thought that, I felt Him say in a kind, playful tone, "Wait a minute . . . what'd you just say?" as if He were stopping me in my tracks to say, "I can do that too."

It caught my attention, so I said, "Okay!" I asked to be done by Tuesday, and when the following Tuesday came, I was finished with all the work for my four classes. It was so exciting to experience this deeper level of His love and desire to bless me. Our Father in heaven loves to give us the things we ask for. It is His delight to bless us and give us good things. Our Father knows our desires and loves to fulfill them. When you ask the Father for something, He will give it to you! All you have to do is believe that He will give it to you.

Questioning the Providence of God

God provides for our desires, but He also provides for our needs. Philippians 2:14 AMP says, **"Do everything without murmuring or questioning [the providence of God]."** This verse gives us a very encouraging command in how we go about our daily activities and how we conduct ourselves. The verse starts by encouraging us against having a negative, complaining attitude. We are encouraged to not go around grumbling, complaining, and murmuring in the things we do, but to trust that the Lord has everything covered through His providence. I like to pronounce this word "provide-ence" emphasizing the word *provide*. The Lord is saying that He will provide for you. Pronouncing the word this way helps you hear that He is saying that He will provide for you.

The verse encourages us to trust and be fully secure, never questioning that the Lord will provide what you need. It is a confidence in His providence that is so secure, you never need to look at the negative side or fearful side, because you know that He has it covered. When you get in a car and are driving down the highway, you never worry or fear that you are going to fall out the side of the car, because you know the door is secure and will not fail. This is how God wants us to feel about His provision. It is so secure that it will not fail.

Many arguments, fears, and worries we face during our day would simply disappear if we trusted that our generous, loving, thoughtful Father in heaven will provide what we need. Think about the fear you have around something you have been considering, or something that you do out of worry or fear, or that you don't like doing, such as always using a cover on your table. Perhaps you like using the actual tabletop when you eat at your dining table, but you are afraid that instead of the table lasting twenty years, you will have to buy a new table after only ten. This is a fear; that isn't trusting that God will provide that wonderful new table when you need it. The fear is "I need to get the most use out of this; *otherwise*, it is wrong that I buy a new one." You feel shame in not doing every possible thing to optimize the usage in fear that you won't have the money for it or out of your shame that makes you feel that you are disentitled to a new table. But we have learned that that shame is a feeling from the enemy and is not founded in God's truths. In both feelings, the providence of God is being questioned: either God doesn't provide the money for a new table, or He simply doesn't even provide the table. But we know that both those fears are lies. We know that God loves to bless us and give us good things that make our lives full, such as with the new table. We see in Philippians 2:14 that He wants us to always trust that He will provide what we need in any situation: the new table, the money, the new plates, the car, the emotional stability we need. He will always provide what you need. So, look at His providence, not the problem, fear, or worry. Look at His providence.

Prosperity

The Lord wants to bless you and provide for you in *every way*. He wants to show you and me every one of His benefits; this includes financial blessing and provision. Another inheritance we have been given by our Heavenly Father though His riches in glory is financial prosperity. Prosperity is something He has freely given to us for us to choose to believe and receive. Often, though, we are fooled into thinking that this is not a thing we can receive, or we believe that there are limits on this prosperity.

One day the Lord showed me His blessing of financial provision. He told me that I would always have the money to eat out whenever I wanted to. This was wonderful to hear and gave me a cheerful heart. Eating out was something that I felt like I wasn't really allowed to do due to the cost. But His statement freed me from that feeling. A couple of weeks later, I had eaten out twice and thought, "Oh, I can't eat out again," as if it were wrong. I felt this reluctance to eat out again stemming from the feeling that I wasn't allowed to spend money. But I felt the Lord nudge me and say, "I told you, you can eat out whenever you'd like." I felt Him in my Spirit saying, "Don't put limits on my blessing." This moment of refocusing on what He had already said to me and on the truth healed that place in my heart that felt like I couldn't spend money, realigning my thoughts and feelings with His promise and blessing.

Prosperity is one of the riches that He has gifted us, and all we must do is lean into it. We are His sons and daughters, and He loves to bless us extravagantly, abundantly, and exceedingly. Matthew 13:8–17 gives us a picture of how we might respond when God gives us a free gift like prosperity:

> **"Other seeds fell on good soil and produced grain, some a hundredfold, some sixty, some thirty. He who has ears, let him hear." Then the disciples came and said to him, "Why do you speak to them in parables?" And he answered them, "To you it has been given to know the secrets of the kingdom of heaven, but to them it has not been given. For to the one who has, more will be given, and he will have an abundance, but from the one who has not, even what he has will be taken away. This is why I speak to them in parables, because seeing they do not see, and hearing they do not hear, nor do they understand. Indeed, in their case the prophecy of Isaiah is fulfilled that says: 'You will indeed hear but never understand, and you will indeed see but never perceive.' For this people's heart has grown dull, and with their ears they can barely hear, and their eyes they have closed, lest they should see with their eyes and hear with their ears and understand with their heart and**

turn, and I would heal them. But blessed are your eyes, for they see, and your ears, for they hear. For truly, I say to you, many prophets and righteous people longed to see what you see, and did not see it, and to hear what you hear, and did not hear it."

Verse 8 talked about the seed. This seed represents His words, and the good soil represents a receptive heart, one that believes what He has said and stands firm in it. Together, they show us what it is like when we receive the words the Lord has spoken over us. It says that when His words are received by a heart that believes what He has said and stands firm in it, that because of this confidence in His word, it produces abundance! When we believe the words of our Father and that the blessings He has given us are real and unending, we allow those blessings to become fruitful in our lives. Our Father would like us to receive His benefits and prosperity with receptive hearts that stand firm in this freedom.

Verse 9 then tells us that this position is the attitude of someone who hears—someone who hears the things the Lord has said and internalizes them. In verses 10 through 12, Jesus explains to us that as children of God, we get to explore all the wonderful things God has to show us. In that place of discovering, exploring, and living in the new dimensions of His freedom, it says that we will experience more and more abundance. The more we seek out what our Father has to show us, the more He will show us, and it will be more fruitful than we can imagine. It is only when we stop believing in Him and trusting Him that we don't experience the wonderfulness of all His benefits and secrets of heaven. Our life comes from Him, and it sucks the life out of us when that connection is impaired. He has abundance for you, and He can't wait to show you! Open your heart to receive the blessing of prosperity He has for you. When you open your heart to receive and confidently stand on His blessing of prosperity, it will become fruitful and abundant in your life.

The next verses, 13 through 15a, show us that sometimes when God gives us a word of abundance and life, we are closed off to it. Our hearts become dull and non-receiving when we stop believing and trusting what the Lord has said. This can happen when we think that God is unfaithful or lean into doubt. But we learned in earlier chapters that God's desire for us is that we would always experience His goodness and benefits. This is our inheritance in Him. You can trust that this is what He has in store for you. You can trust that if you believe what He has spoken to you, it will come to pass. Unbelief and doubt are the only things that can rob what He has spoken over you of its power.

Sometimes we stop believing and trusting simply because we don't think what He said is possible. But as we've learned, God's definition of what can happen is not tied to what the world deems as possible. We are freed from the world's perspectives and are invited to receive the perspectives of heaven through the lens of Jesus's Resurrection. What God says is available to us is possible, because we live in the fullness of who He is and in the fullness of all His benefits. Our lives are not dictated by the way the world works. We operate in the fullness of heaven and Jesus's Resurrection. And when we look at things through this new life Jesus has given us, everything He has said becomes possible.

The wonderful news is that in the rest of verse 15, it says that even in your places of dullness of heart, Jesus is standing right there next to you, waiting for you to turn your heart to Him and to choose to receive what He has spoken to you. And when you do, it says that He will heal that place in your heart, and you will be able to receive the wonderful thing He wants to give you. Let the Lord heal the places in your heart where you have become dull to receiving His prosperity in your life.

Jesus finishes this thought with verses 16 and 17, in which He speaks a blessing over us when we receive what He is doing, saying, and giving. He says that our eyes are blessed because we see what He is doing, and our ears are blessed because we hear what He is saying. He says that many others have longed and desired to see the wonderful glory that we get to live in. We can live in these things because we are open to receiving the wonderful benefits and treasures the Lord has for us. The Lord is breaking open His glory over us, and it is our quest to receive and discover all these things. The Lord says that we are blessed when we recognize and receive what He is doing and saying; we are blessed when we receive His prosperity over our lives.

He is breaking prosperity open over us, and His call to us is that we would have a receptive, believing heart toward the prosperity He has given to us to live in. Our Father wants us to fully dive deep into all His blessings and to fully enjoy and live in His prosperity.

Heavenly Treasures

Colossians 3:2 (TPT) shows us that we are to focus on the realities of heaven, such as His unfailing providence, and not on the things in this earthly realm that would steal the wonderful blessings and inheritances we have because we are citizens of heaven: **"Yes, feast on all the treasures of the heavenly realm and fill your thoughts with heavenly realities, and not with the distractions of the natural realm."** We are called to a higher level. We are called to interact with Jesus, the Father, and the Holy Spirit on a level that is beyond what we see in front of us. What we see in front of us is not our reality anymore. Jesus, the Father, and the Holy Spirit call us into their heavenly realm. They call us to see what they see, hear what they hear, and experience all the riches, treasures, blessings, and benefits Jesus bought on the cross for us. We are called to feast, to feast on the treasures of the heavenly realm!

That reference to "feast" is a powerful indulgent phrase. It is a level of abundance where you have so much more than you could possibly contain, so much excellence and glory. We are called and invited to fill our minds with heavenly realities—the realities of His providence, His desire to fill our desires, and His prosperity, the reality that fear, worry, and shame don't have a say over our lives anymore. And we are called to not focus on our reality that we see in front of us. Jesus has everything you could ever want, in a level of abundance you couldn't imagine. Jesus wants you to walk with Him and have Him teach you about heaven's realities and about all that He bought for you on the cross.

This is our journey, discovering all of the things and all the deeper levels of what He has bought for us to experience. It is a journey of relationship and discovery beyond anything you could've ever imagined. So feast on what Jesus has said is available to you, and ask Him to show you more deeper levels of His abundance.

Freedom with Food

Another area that Jesus provided freedom in is with food. Colossians 2:20–23 says:

> **If with Christ you died to the elemental spirits of the world, why, as if you were still alive in the world, do you submit to regulations—Do not handle, Do not taste, Do not touch (referring to things that all perish as they are used)— according to human precepts and teachings? These have indeed an appearance of wisdom in promoting self-made religion and asceticism and severity to the body, but they are of no value in stopping the indulgence of the flesh.**

This verse gives us quite a neat heavenly perspective. We are shown here that we are allowed to eat all foods. We are called up into the heavenly reality in this verse that we no longer have regulations around what we can eat now that we are in Christ. Since we are no longer of the world and are now in Christ, we don't have to live by these rules and regulations that say a particular food is bad or harmful. Those rules and regulations are inspired by the elemental spirits that control this world, and they do not come from God. We are alive in Christ and can live outside those rules.

The passage goes on in verse 23 to tell us that these rules and regulations seem like wisdom, but they are not our reality. They come from the broken ways the world functions, but we no longer function this way. Because they have the appearance of wisdom, these rules and regulations can seem undeniable and so certain that we couldn't reject them, but we can reject them, because we are not bound by the cause and effect designed by this world. Verse 23 shows us that these rules and regulations were not how God intended for you and your body to live and result in regulations that our Father in heaven never meant for us to live under. We are freed from a way of living where we aren't allowed to enjoy food. Jesus freed us from this on the cross, and it is one of His many benefits that we get to live in!

The world around us would say that listening to the research about why different foods harm you and why you shouldn't eat them is good and wise, but this verse warns us that this is not wisdom and we should not listen to them. Our Father did not design our bodies to be deprived of certain kinds of food. He designed food for us to enjoy. This way of thinking is a heavenly reality, believing that God created food for us and that we can enjoy all food fully, despite what anyone would say about that being wrong. It is a distraction of the world to say that we must be careful about what we eat or that we can't eat certain things. We are meant to function differently than the world around us, and that includes food. Jesus's freedom extends to food. We are meant to be free with food. It is a blatant lie of the enemy to say that some food is bad or that you can't enjoy it.

The second half of verse 23 shows us that if we choose to obey these rules, it is self-made religion—but God is meant to be our source, not ourselves. The verse references it as asceticism, which means regularly or permanently depriving yourself of a food or other things for religious reasons[1]—but God said that all food is good and that He loves to give us good things. The verse says that these rules are severity to the body—but God said to be gentle and that all food was made for us to eat and enjoy. We can be confident that it is good when we enjoy all foods. Jesus has given us this freedom and heavenly treasure, so feast on it!

In Colossians 2:2–4, Paul gives us this admonition:

That their hearts may be encouraged, being knit together in love, to reach all the riches of full assurance of understanding and the knowledge of God's mystery, which is Christ, in whom are hidden all the treasures of wisdom and knowledge. I say this in order that no one may delude you with plausible arguments.

Paul is warning us that as we are looking to discover the mysteries, wisdom, and knowledge of Jesus's Resurrection, we should not listen to the plausible arguments people will pose against us. The world and the enemy will come to you with persuasive arguments that feel undeniable, but Paul is telling us to not believe these arguments. For example, we do not have to believe the world's argument that "Some food is bad, and here is the proof." This is a plausible argument. *We are not bound* by the way the world works. We are free! We are free in Christ. We are free from the boundaries and dysfunctions sin and death put on us. The ways of sin and death would say, "This thing interacts improperly with your body, so don't eat it." But Paul is telling us here that we are a new creation in Christ, and because of that, this rationale no longer applies to us. We are invited to live in the alignment that Christ created, and that alignment states that food, a good thing the Lord created for us to enjoy, no longer has a right to interact improperly with our bodies.

It is a false lie of the enemy to say that the rule of sin and death that states food is bad still applies to us. It doesn't. When we came alive in Jesus's Resurrection, we were seated with Him in heaven and are invited to live in heavenly realities. You do not have to be bound to the way the world says things are or should be. We were freed from the natural realm's reality. We are instructed to look beyond this world and look through the eyes of Jesus's Resurrection. Paul tells us this same thing in Galatians 5:7–8: **"You were running well. Who hindered you from obeying the truth? This persuasion is not from him who calls you."** We have been given freedom! Don't forget these freedoms and benefits the Lord has for you. Do not let the world or the enemy tell you with persuasive arguments that you cannot live in them. We have been given many freedoms, and the Lord's desire is that we would live in them to the fullest! Don't be persuaded out of the heavenly freedoms Jesus has given us: our freedom with food, our freedom with healing, our freedom with prosperity. Live in them with heavenly conviction.

David tells us in Psalm 103:2–5 to not forget the wonderful benefits that the Lord has given us:

Bless the Lord, O my soul, and forget not all his benefits, who forgives all your iniquity, who heals all your diseases, who redeems your life from the pit, who crowns you with steadfast love and mercy, who satisfies you with good so that your youth is renewed like the eagle's.

Remember these freedoms, blessings, and benefits. Do not let these freedoms be stolen from you or for your heart and mind to become dull to where you forget the wonderful things we have been invited to live in. They are your rightful inheritance as a child of God. The Lord has supplied us with so much good, and He invites us to live in it, to experience it, to feast on it. This is what Jesus died on the cross to give us. This is who Jesus is. So do not let the world's arguments or the enemy's persuasion lead you away from all the wonderful benefits the Lord has given you.

Paul tells us in Philippians 3:16 that as our Father is showing us all the wonderful things He has given us that we are to hold true to what we have learned and discovered: **"Only let us hold true to what we have attained."** Our Father in heaven is continually showing us new levels of the freedom and blessing He has supplied for us, and this verse encourages us to hold fast to those things, to remember them, live in them, and to make them a part of us. This is what living in heavenly realities is like. It is holding onto the freedoms that Jesus has given us, and it is living in these freedoms. Living and thinking in this way is what it is like to have the mind of Christ. The Lord has given us freedom in everything, so let's live in it.

CHAPTER 6

Women and Marriages

Another area of our lives that Jesus gave us freedom in is in our relationships, particularly the relationship between a husband and a wife. But before we explore the freedom He has given us in that relationship, let's look at how God views women.

How God Views Women

In **Galatians 3:28,** God tells us a little bit about what He thinks about women: **"There is neither Jew nor Greek, there is neither slave nor free, there is no male and female, for you are all one in Christ Jesus."** This verse highlights the way God uses people and sees people. He is saying that He doesn't judge and distinguish on the bases of race, status, or gender. He states here that men and women are equal, and He uses them equally. He shows us in this verse that women are not less than men in the kingdom of God, and He does not say that men can do one thing and women another. We are all one in Christ. Male dominance—the idea that men have a higher position or that women have a lesser position in the kingdom of God—was one of the effects of sin and death that we were freed from. God's desire is that we would be one, be equal, and be free. This male dominance is a function of the world, but we are free from the world and its laws. It is a false dichotomy and a distortion of the enemy to say that men have a higher position in God's eyes and that women have a lesser position. This is an attempt of the enemy to hold us in bondage. Our Father in heaven does not cut off His daughters. The Bible says that Jesus died for freedom. He gave freedom to women. You, Woman of God, do not have to live and believe that you are cut off from the things of God. God wants to use you and give you all His abundance. You are not less, and He does not cut you off. He gave you freedom from being told and living like you are less. You have been given freedom! You are free!

In Ephesians 2:14–15 (NASB), we are shown that the dividing wall between men and women has been taken down. It was broken down:

> **For He Himself is our peace, who made both *groups into* one and broke down the barrier of the dividing wall, by abolishing in His flesh the enmity, *which is* the Law of commandments *contained* in ordinances, so that in Himself He might make the two into one new man, *thus* establishing peace.**

Jesus gave us peace between all of us when He died and rose again. This includes breaking the dividing wall between men and women. He did not say that everyone is included except for women. He gave peace to the division between men and women and stated that we are now one in Christ. This was His original design. It is persuasion of the enemy to say that there is division between men and women. There is no division—Jesus destroyed it and made us one. He has given us this freedom to live in in this very moment, and it is only when we listen to plausible arguments and the persuasion of the enemy that we allow this freedom to be stolen from us. But Jesus's desire is that you would turn to Him and live in this freedom and when you do, He will show you more amazing things than you could've ever imagined. Jesus tore down the division between men and women and made us whole again, made us one again. We are free, and we are one.

Another effect of sin and death that this verse shows us is broken through Jesus's Resurrection is where it says that enmity is abolished. We learned in chapter 3 (through the Genesis 3 passage) that enmity between the enemy and women was one of the effects of sin and death. This word *enmity* means opposition and hostility. When sin entered the world in the Garden of Eden, there was a direct assignment of the enemy against women. But Jesus in this verse is saying that that assignment is now broken; that enmity is gone. The assignment of the enemy against women is broken, and women are now free from all that opposition. Jesus freed us by abolishing the enmity on the cross with His body. Let us live it.

We honor Jesus's sacrifice by living in this freedom that He died for and rose for! This is the deep, deep desire of His heart: for us to live in the freedom of His Resurrection. He shows us time and time again that women are free, male dominance is gone, and enmity is abolished. Now *we* need to receive this freedom and walk in it. We have peace; we have freedom. Women no longer have to walk in the shadow of men—this shadow that was created by the enemy, not our Father. Women are free to be who they were created to be and to interact on a level playing field with men.

Paul gives us a neat picture of the redemption of women in 1 Timothy 2:13–15:

> **For Adam was formed first, then Eve; and Adam was not deceived, but the woman was deceived and became a transgressor. Yet she will be saved through childbearing—if they continue in faith and love and holiness, with self-control.**

Verses 13 and 14, when read alone, can sound harsh and sound like Paul is demeaning women. But when you pair verses 13 and 14 with verse 15, you can see that Paul is showing us a picture of what women have lived under and what they are now invited into in Christ. Verses 13 and 14 recount the failure Eve as a woman had in the Garden of Eden when she chose sin over God. But after this statement, Paul adds in this word—*yet*—which means "despite my previous statement."

Paul says here that despite this failure women had in the Garden of Eden, they could be redeemed and that redemption was childbearing, which is the birth of Christ, born of a woman. Women are saved and redeemed by Jesus and through their faith in Him.

The mistake Eve made in the Garden is no longer held against the daughters of God because Jesus came and fixed everything and redeemed women. God does not look at women as less than. He looks at them as redeemed and fully restored.

Wives and Husbands

And it is in this freedom that Jesus gave radical freedom and change to the husband-wife relationship. In Colossians 3, we are given a beautiful description of how our relationship with Christ is reflected in our relationships with our spouses. Verse 18 of chapter 3 focuses on the reflection of one's relationship with Christ through the woman. Colossians 3:18 (TPT) reads, **"Let every wife be supportive and tenderly devoted to her husband, *for this is a beautiful illustration* of our devotion to Christ."** This verse is showing a reflection of Christ through the wife onto the husband. When Jesus interacts with us, He supports and upholds us. Jesus is also tenderly devoted to us. We see this through the way He loves us, chases after us, never leaves us, walks with us, and stands with us. This is devotion. This is how wives demonstrate Christ to their husbands.

Verse 19 focuses on the reflection of the husband's relationship with Christ onto his wife. Colossians 3:19 (TPT) reads, **"Let every husband be filled with cherishing love for his wife and never be insensitive toward her."** A husband loves and demonstrates Jesus to his wife by showing her cherishing love. This deep love of a husband for his wife expresses Christ in a deep way to her. This type of love is the same love Christ has for us, which He demonstrated through

His death on the cross and through the many ways He blesses and cares for us. Jesus is also sensitive toward us and is never harsh, rude, or rough. This gentleness, kindness, and sensitivity is another way a husband demonstrates Jesus to his wife. These kinds of interactions and reflections of Christ are how our Father in heaven designed the husband-wife relationship to be. He designed this relationship to reflect how He treats us.

Jesus, through His Resurrection, realigned and healed the husband-wife relationship. Through His Resurrection, Jesus broke the enemy's assignment that set out to push women down and restrict them, whether that was in their position in the church or in their marriages. When sin entered the world in the Garden of Eden, the husband-wife relationship became distorted because of this enemy assignment and because of the effect of sin and death, which states that husbands will rule over their wives. But this power balance shift that sin and death instigated between husbands and wives—in which they would try to topple each other in power, rather than be in harmony and be seen as equal with one another—is something that Jesus realigned and gave us freedom in through His Resurrection. Jesus overturned and abolished all the laws of sin and death, and this brokenness in the husband-wife relationship was one of the things Jesus healed.

This lens of Jesus's healing and realignment is how we are to look at the husband-wife relationship. I am not going to look at every verse about husbands and wives in this book, but it is important that we look at those verses through the new lens Jesus gave us. If we look at such verses through the old lenses of sin and death, we will always misinterpret what Jesus is wanting to show us. Jesus abolished the enemy's assignment over women, and He healed the division that sin and death placed between husbands and wives: this is the lens through which we are to look at this relationship. Jesus restored the husband-wife relationship to be one of harmony and equality.

CHAPTER 7

Other Areas of Freedom (Part 2)

Holding This World in Bondage

Jesus, the Father, and the Holy Spirit have taught and shown us many of the kinds of freedoms Jesus has bought for us through His Resurrection. In Ephesians 6:12 (TPT), they also show us a little bit of the enemy's strategy against us in this journey:

> **Your hand-to-hand combat is not with human beings, but with the highest principalities and authorities operating in rebellion under the heavenly realms. For they are a powerful class of demon-gods and evil spirits that hold this dark world in bondage.**

The words I want to focus on in this verse are in the last phrase, where it says that evil spirits hold this world in bondage.

We know that we have been freed by Christ from everything that holds this world in bondage. So then why do we still fall into the rhythms of this world that seem to limit our freedom? This is because the enemy holds this world in bondage, and he tries to re-ensnare us into thinking we are also under the bondages of this world. The enemy's goal is to keep us and this world in bondage; and to do this he comes to us with lies and persuasions. This is our fight against the enemy. His goal is to keep us in bondage, but as we learn all the areas of freedom Jesus has given us and learn to identify and break out of the bondages that the enemy uses, we begin to fully live in our freedom.

This verse also tells us that the daily things we fight within this world are not what they seem; they are not the tangible things before our eyes. This verse tells us that these things originate from the enemy, sin, and death, and that this is the angle that we are to attack them from. When we look at our problems from the angle that they originate from the enemy, sin, and death, our ability to overcome them becomes far more tangible and realizable, since we have been given every authority over the enemy, sin, and death and are no longer under any of their power. We are free from all the plans of the enemy and have been given power, freedom, and confidence through our Father, Jesus, and the Holy Spirit. We have been given power by Jesus to take authority over all the things in our lives that stand in opposition to Jesus's Resurrection and would be less than the freedom He bought for us.

Stress-Free Life

The Lord has freed us from every type of bondage, so don't be persuaded to fall back into that bondage. Stress is one of the bondages that the enemy tries to keep us in, but Jesus has provided everything you need for you to live in peace and security. The Lord has taught us to live a life where we trust in Him; a life where we trust that He will provide for our finances and our emotions; a life where we have confidence in His goodness and His desire to bless us; a life where He has said that if we ask, He will give. So why would there be a need to live in stress when we know that Jesus has provided everything that we need before we need it?

He looks on you with joy and excitement. Rest in His joy and excitement over you. You don't have to fear a possibility or an outcome; you don't have to fear any kind of lack—lack of clothing or lack of time. You are free in Christ, and He has provided a life for you where you do not have to feel stressed, but where you can rest in Him and His provision. You can rest in His joy. This is where your strength comes from. You can rest in the joy and enjoyment He has given you.

You do not have to stress or fear; He has called you to be a son or daughter whose confidence is in their Father. Why would I stress and fear when I have a Father who cares so deeply and is ordering my every step in cherishing, thoughtful love? We have every reason to be in peace, estranged to fear, because of our confidence in our Father who cares deeply for each of us. Walk in the confidence of your Father, and do not fear. He is with you, walking beside you, laughing with you as you go, and because you are so deep in His love for you, nothing else can make it through that barrier. Walk in this way, this peaceful way, where you are full of life abundant.

Worry-Free Life

It is from a place of confidence and trust in Him that we can live a life without worry. When we trust in His care and providence for us in every way, the need for worry disappears because we have security in Him. This security is trustworthy and will not fail. The Lord always plans the best for you, and you can rely on His care for you. He cares about the clothing you need and the finances you need. He cares about your wants and desires; He cares about all the things in your life out of a deep love for you.

This love is reliable. This love sustains you. This love supplies you with all you need. When we lean and rest on the love of our God, we can take a posture of thankfulness that focuses on the wonderful things He has given us to live in right now. We no longer have a need to worry. Worry comes from the enemy in an attempt to steal your trust and confidence in the Lord, but we have certain confidence in the Lord. Worry is incompatible with this trust and with the things the Lord has gifted to us.

The enemy would try to keep us in bondage to worry, but we have no need to worry because our Father has provided everything we need. It is a heavenly reality to say that worry no longer has a right over us because we now live in the kingdom of heaven, where our Father has said He has everything for us. Worry isn't a thing we are meant to function under. Jesus defeated worry through His Resurrection on the cross, releasing all of heaven over us. All the abundance of the Kingdom of Christ is open over us! Don't listen to the lie of worry. Worry is a lie and a veil the enemy tries to hang over our eyes, but it has no gravity. The Lord's provision has gravity in our lives. Because of Jesus's Resurrection, worry has lost its power. And now *we* can take up the power of our Father's provision. Walk in an unbreakable confidence in the Lord's care and provision and in the belief that worry can't touch you. You are free in Christ!

Sons of God

Jesus bought freedom for everyone and everything. The freedom Jesus bought that extends to us also extends to the whole of creation on the earth. We learned in chapter 3 that Jesus broke the authority of weeds, but in that moment, He also bestowed life and freedom, similarly to how He broke sin and death but also gave us life and freedom. Romans 8:18–23 is an incredibly neat passage of scripture that shows us that this freedom Jesus bought for us extends not only to us, but also to all of creation:

> **For I consider that the sufferings of this present time are not worth comparing with the glory that is to be revealed to us. For the creation waits with eager longing for the revealing of the sons of God. For the creation was subjected to futility, not willingly, but because of him who subjected it, in hope that the creation itself will be set free from its bondage to corruption and**

obtain the freedom of the glory of the children of God. For we know that the whole creation has been groaning together in the pains of childbirth until now. And not only the creation, but we ourselves, who have the firstfruits of the Spirit, groan inwardly as we wait eagerly for adoption as sons, the redemption of our bodies.

This passage is full of neat statements, and the first is in verse 18: **"For I consider that the sufferings of this present time are not worth comparing with the glory that is to be revealed to us."** The Greek word used for time in this verse is *kairós*, and it refers to an opportune time, a suitable time, a favorable moment, and a time when "things are coming to a head to take full advantage of".[1] We are living in a time that the Lord would call opportune and favorable. That is exciting! This description shows us that the Lord has something extremely special in this time for us to take full advantage of, unlike any other time before. The Lord is calling out the uniqueness and specialness of the time we are in, and He calls us to take full advantage of it! This is the kind of time that we are living in. The second half of verse 18 tells us that during this kairós time, there is an incredible glory that is going to be revealed to us.

When this idea of glory being revealed to us is paired with 2 Corinthians 3:18 (NASB) we are given a neat picture of what this time of discovering glory is like: **"But we all with unveiled face, beholding as in a mirror the glory of the Lord, are being transformed into the same image from *glory to glory*, just as from the Lord, the spirit"** (italics mine). We are living in a time when we are constantly discovering the incredible glory the Lord has for us. We are living in a time when Jesus desires that we would take full advantage of His glory that He has given us. We are living in a favorable time and a time of opportunity. Every day, we are invited to discover more aspects of His glory that He has gifted to us. He gave us this glory for us to experience and take full advantage of. This is His desire.

But then Jesus takes it a step further in verses 19 through 22 of the Romans 8 passage:

> **For the creation waits with eager longing for the revealing of the sons of God. For the creation was subjected to futility, not willingly, but because of him who subjected it, in hope that the creation itself will be set free from its bondage to corruption and obtain the freedom of the glory of the children of God. For we know that the whole creation has been groaning together in the pains of childbirth until now.**

Up till this moment, Jesus has showed us how He has given us His glory and how we are invited to live in it because of His Resurrection. He has shown us the great extent of His glory to all the areas of our lives and of the great expanse of His glory that goes beyond any boundaries that sin and death may have set. It is a boundless glory. But now in verses 19 through 22, He takes this glory beyond us and extends it to *all of creation*. Verse 19 says that creation is waiting in eager longing for the revealing of the sons of God.

The Bible would tell us that anyone who believes in Jesus and His Resurrection is considered a son of God. This verse makes a distinction that when we come into our full right as sons of God and fully function in His glory that He has given us and is revealing to us, not only we but *everything on earth* is impacted. Verses 20 and 21 say that when sin and death entered the world, creation became subjected to sin and death, but that creation had hope, and that hope was that creation itself would be set free from its bondage to corruption (which comes from sin and death) and obtain the glory of the children of God. God has given us incredible glory. But now in this passage, Jesus shows us that when we function in this glory, that this freedom from all of sin and death extends to all of creation: all the people, plants, animals, and everything else. Jesus not only freed us but all of creation through His Resurrection.

Verse 21 says that all of creation has been groaning, waiting for the moment that the sons of God would be revealed *until now*. This groaning has stopped. Jesus's Resurrection broke the power of sin and death everywhere—over us, over the grass, over the trees, over everything. Sin does not have a hold over this earth anymore. This picture of freedom that Jesus has given us is much like the movie *The Matrix* in that what we see in front of us is not reality. It is a false picture that tries to hold us in bondage and corruption. But when we realize that we are not bound by this reality that we see, we can bend the spoon like the little boy does in the movie and live in all the freedoms of this glory and Jesus's Resurrection. When we realize that sin and death are no longer of power and no longer have a right to affect our lives, we can live fully free.

And this freedom we can extend to the people, plants, and animals around us.

With the inclusion of verse 23, this entire six-verse passage gives us a picture of the three-part sanctification we go through. The three-part sanctification is: (1) we were saved when we believed in Jesus's Resurrection, (2) we are also being saved daily by growing and becoming like Jesus, and (3) we will also have a final sanctification at the Second Coming of Jesus.

We were fully given glory when we accepted Jesus, and through His Resurrection, the groaning of creation and the power of sin and death ceased, but we are also being transformed from glory to glory as we walk out our lives and learn to live in this glory and freedom. Finally, in verse 23, it gives us the last piece and shows our final sanctification: **"And not only the creation, but we ourselves, who have the firstfruits of the Spirit, groan inwardly as we wait eagerly for adoption as sons, the redemption of our bodies."** This verse begins with the second part of sanctification that we are experiencing in the Spirit now. Then the verse continues on to say that we are eagerly waiting for the redemption of our bodies.

The word here for "wait eagerly" in the Greek is *apekdechómenoi*, and it means to "welcome from and out of." [2] It is a kind of waiting that is active; it is not passive. It is actively moving into something and away from another thing. We are moving away from the functions of sin and death and into the glory and freedoms of Jesus's Resurrection. This fits very well with the idea that we are in a kairós time to take full advantage of the glory Jesus has given us as we move from glory to glory.

At the end of verse 23, the Greek word *sóma* is translated to "bodies." In other translations, it is listed as "body" because sóma is the word used to refer to the *body* of Christ.[3] The very end of this verse is illuding to our third and final sanctification at the Second Coming of Jesus, where the body of Christ will be fully redeemed.

Discovery

We are shown many times in Scripture that Jesus's Resurrection goes beyond simply being saved and going to heaven. There is a constant theme in Scripture that calls us to search out and experience the endless treasures of His Resurrection: all His benefits, His immeasurable greatness, the riches of our glorious inheritance, and the full power of Jesus's Resurrection. Jesus's desire is that we would recognize all these wonderful things He bought for us on the cross and that we would live in them. Ephesians 1:16b–21 gives us a picture of what this discovery looks like:

> **Remembering you in my prayers, that the God of our Lord Jesus Christ, the Father of glory, may give you the Spirit of wisdom and of revelation in the knowledge of him, having the eyes of your hearts enlightened, that you may know what is the hope to which he has called you, what are the riches of his glorious inheritance in the saints, and what is the immeasurable greatness of his power toward us who believe, according to the working of his great might that he worked in Christ when he**

raised him from the dead and seated him at his right hand in the heavenly places, far above all rule and authority and power and dominion, and above every name that is named, not only in this age but also in the one to come.

Verse 17 reads like a declaration over us. It is a declaration that we would have the Spirit of revelation and that we would have enlightened hearts, not hearts that have grown dull to the wonderful benefits we have in Christ. We have been called to live in abundant life, full of the power of Jesus. We are called to know and discover the riches of His glorious inheritance in us and of the immeasurable greatness of His power.

This Spirit of revelation then gets paired with the Spirit of wisdom. The Spirit of wisdom is the active walking out of what we now know. It is actually doing and experiencing the things we've learned.[1] The Lord's desire is that we would not stop at simply knowing that we have freedom, but that we would actually fully experience it!

The Lord says in these verses that this same power He calls us to know and experience is the same power that not only raised Jesus from the dead, but also sat Him in a place of authority beyond anything and everything. This is an incredible kind of power that our Lord has given us to know, experience, and function in. Jesus desires that we would take full advantage of the power that He has given us to live in. It is a kind of power that is absolute and has no equal. This allows us to have a confidence in Jesus, the Father, and the Holy Spirit unlike anything else because their power is unfailing and unbreakable. This is the kind of power Jesus calls us to experience and take full advantage of. What a calling!

Paul tells us in Ephesians 3:8 (NLT) that we are to explore the endless treasures available to us in Christ: **"Though I am the least deserving of all God's people, he graciously gave me the privilege of telling the Gentiles about the endless treasures available to them in Christ."** We have endless treasures in Christ! Jesus gave us endless treasures! We are in a kairós time of discovering these treasures and taking full advantage of them! Enjoy these endless treasures, and let Holy Spirit reveal each one of them to you.

Paul shows us another picture of this discovery in Philippians 3:9–11:

> **And be found in him, not having a righteousness of my own that comes from the law, but that which comes through faith in Christ, the righteousness from God that depends on faith—that I may know him and the power of his resurrection, and may share his sufferings, becoming like him in his death, that by any means possible I may attain the resurrection from the dead.**

Verse 10 shows us that our focus is on knowing Jesus deeper and knowing His power in a deeper way. We were saved by Jesus but are now called to discover more of Him in relationship and to discover the full extent of His power. This is our call.

The end of verse 10 and verse 11 show us again the picture of what it looks like to move out of sin and death and into the power of Jesus's Resurrection: (1) we are becoming like Jesus in His death—Jesus defeated sin and death through His death, and now we are partnering with that victory and are coming out from under the functions of sin and death, and (2) we are attaining the Resurrection from the dead—we are raised to life with Christ and are moving into the power and benefits of Jesus's Resurrection. Our journey is to have deeper relationship with Jesus and then to learn about and experience His incredible power.

Lastly, in Colossians 3:1 Paul gives us this neat statement: **"If then you have been raised with Christ, seek the things that are above, where Christ is, seated at the right hand of God."** We were separated from sin and death and were raised to abundant life with Christ. In this place of abundant life, we are called to seek the things of heaven and of Christ. Jesus has been given all dominion, authority, and ultimate power. Sin and death are no longer controlling powers over us. Jesus took away their authority over us and crowned us with all the things of His kingdom, the kingdom of ultimate power, dominion, and authority. This is the kingdom we get to share and live in. So explore with the Father, Jesus, and the Holy Spirit all the wonderful things they have for you to discover and live in. The kingdom of heaven is our reality!

CHAPTER 8

Foundations of the New Era

Love Is the Basis

We have entered a new era and the Lord is inviting us to begin a fresh journey of discovery. One thing that is critical to this journey of discovery with Jesus, the Holy Spirit, and the Father is love. We are shown in the New Testament a parallel between our journey of discovery and our increase in love. Philippians 1:9–11 (NASB) reads:

> **And this I pray, that your love may abound still more and more in real knowledge and all discernment, so that you may approve the things that are excellent, in order to be sincere and blameless until the day of Christ; having been filled with the fruit of righteousness which**

comes **through Jesus Christ, to the glory and praise of God.**

Let's also look at verse 9 in The Passion Translation version (TPT): **"I continue to pray for your love to grow and increase beyond measure, bringing you into the rich revelation of spiritual insight in all things."** This passage draws a connection between our journey of discovery and our level of love. There is an importance to continually increase in love while you discover all the freedoms and inheritances we have in Christ. Jesus died and rose for us out of love. It was through that love that our freedoms came. As we are called to share in Jesus's death and in His Resurrection, we are called to share in this great love. As you go each day personally walking and discovering with Jesus the things He has bought for you out of love, as you feel the love and gentleness He has toward you and choose to fully experience this love, your love will also increase, and your intimacy with the Lord will grow and become deeper. Your ability to function in the power Jesus has given you will also increase as you feel more deeply His heart of love toward you and His significance in you. The more you allow Jesus's love to permeate you, the more you will also grow in love. This combination of great love and discovery is where you can come into the full revelation of who Jesus is. It is here your relationship with Him will be without limits, and you will be able to fully attain His Resurrection.

Ephesians 3:16–19 also shows us this connection between our love and our discovery:

That according to the riches of his glory he may grant you to be strengthened with power through his spirit in your inner being, so that Christ may dwell in your hearts through faith— that you, being rooted and grounded in love, may have strength to comprehend with all the saints what is the depth and length and height and depth, and to know the love of Christ that surpasses knowledge, that you may be filled with all the fullness of God.

Having this strong, deep foundation of love that comes from intimacy with the Lord is the foundation for being filled with the fullness of God. This love that the Lord calls us to is the gateway that allows us to discover all His goodness. We become grounded in love when we allow Jesus to show us His heart of love toward us and His desire for us to experience every one of His riches. When you feel His love and tenderness for you, His love begins to infuse your soul and creates a foundation of love in your spirit and soul, which becomes the basis for how you interact. When you allow His love to go deep inside you, it will change the way you think and see things. It will spill over onto others and into how you do things. This is the picture of what being rooted and grounded in love looks like.

Our ability to discover comes from our willingness to have the mind of Christ, which functions under heavenly realities. Being grounded in this love of Christ transforms your mind and your thoughts to align with heavenly realities. This realignment allows you to discover and be filled with all the fullness of God. Take a moment and feel the love of Christ over you. Let it go deep inside you and warm and comfort you. Let it permeate through your body all the way to your fingertips. Let this love build within your soul as you are close to Him. This deep place of love and tenderness will allow you to discover all the things and clearly see the things the Lord has given to you to experience.

The Power of God and His Protection

It is from this place of deep love with the Lord that we can confidently function in power. Our God is powerful and unmatched. He is the ruling power. He defeated sin completely and abolished death. Sin and death are no longer the ruling powers; our God is, and He has made us co-heirs and co-laborers with Christ, allowing us to share in all He is. When you look at our God of healing and freedom as the ruling power and look at the things of sin and death as lesser, defeated, and powerless, our confidence becomes absolute. It is not hard to have faith and believe when we have this perspective because nothing will ever be stronger than our God. It does not matter what the issue is when it falls under the law of sin and death. We are no longer to adhere to sin and death's ways, bondages, and corruptions. Our God of healing and freedom is the ruling power! You can confidently speak to whatever problem is before you, no matter how long you have had it or how impossible it seems. Those problems all fall under the law of sin and death, and sin and death is not the ruling power anymore. Our God is the ruling power, and we are in Him.

Our God can and will make those high places low and low places high; this is our confidence, and He has given us this same authority. All the power of sin and death has been lost. It is a powerless thing. But we have power, and when we take our place of power in Christ, we can overcome any problem confidently without doubt because sin and death have no power. There is no reason to doubt our ability to overcome and shut down the things of sin and death, because they are already defeated and abolished. And we are now partnered with our God, who is the ruling power. Jesus stole the power of sin and death, released the power and fullness of heaven and our God, and then called us to fully experience and function in every bit of His power. You are in a place of authority with Christ, and sin and death are now subject to *you* as a co-heir with Christ.

When you look at your problems with the mind of Christ and under the lens of heavenly realities, you will be able to clearly see that it is under sin and death and as such no longer has authority; you have the absolute power over it as a citizen of heaven in the kingdom of God. Jesus's desire is that we would fully understand and function in this power. He has undone our shackles to sin and death; now we need to step out of them and take up our place as a son or daughter of God. We have entered a time where the Lord will be showing us all the dimensions of His power and fullness. So let's fall into the deep end of our God and let Him show us *everything* as we continue to be rooted in love.

Jesus has already gone before us and defeated every enemy. We can confidently walk on the path He has prepared for us. We have a God of protection that goes before us. We have nothing to fear. We get to learn and function in all He is, resting in His protection, walking on the smooth way He has prepared for us. Rest in this and enjoy Jesus. Enjoy this journey of Jesus teaching you about Himself and all He has for you. He has already won and prepared the way; now we get to enjoy His victory.

We are being led by our God in power, out of a time where we lived bound by the ways of sin and death. We are coming into a new era where Jesus will be taking us out into the wide open to experience *all* His freedoms and fullness. He is filling us with love and sending us out in power, freedom, and fullness unlike any time before. We are leaving an old, defeated way of living and are entering the new, heavenly filled way of living that we have never before experienced. We will be conquerors in Christ who take territory that the enemy will never again control. And we will experience the freedom and fullness of our God. This is the time we are entering. Have an expectation that the Lord will show you incredible things!

With Other People

As we learn about and experience all the things Jesus bought for us, we are meant to encourage one another in these things and call one another up into the things of Christ. Ephesians 5:19 shows us this: **"Addressing one another in psalms and hymns and spiritual songs, singing and making melody to the Lord with your heart."** The TPT lists the middle portion as, **"Keep speaking to each other with words of Scripture."** We are all meant to experience the fullness of God, and by encouraging one another in the things the Spirit is revealing to us, we can bring others along with us and build one another up in spiritual maturity and in the fullness of God. We are meant to journey together and are meant to be one body that functions together.

Ephesians 2:19–22 (NKJV) shows us a picture of how the body of Christ works together to attain the fullness of Christ:

> **Now, therefore, you are no longer strangers and foreigners, but fellow citizens with the saints and members of the household of God, having been built on the foundation of the apostles and prophets, Jesus Christ Himself being the chief corner*stone*, in whom the whole building, being fitted together, grows into a holy temple in the Lord, in whom you also are being built together for a dwelling place of God in the Spirit.**

Jesus laid the foundation for us to discover all of who He is. Now we are to discover the things of Christ, together. This verse gives us a picture of everyone who is a child of God growing together in Christ to create a wonderful temple that the Lord can dwell in, or in other words, where the fullness of God can dwell in—where everything that He is can dwell. We achieve the fullness of Jesus's Resurrection together. We are one body and grow as one. We bring others along with us and show them the revelations of the Spirit and encourage them to live them out too. We are growing as one body.

Ephesians 4:11–14 (TPT) also shows us a picture of how we grow as one body:

And he has appointed some *with grace* to be apostles, and some *with grace* to be prophets, and some *with grace* to be evangelists, and some *with grace* to be pastors, and some *with grace* to be teachers. And their calling is to nurture and prepare all the holy believers to do their own works of ministry and as they do this they will enlarge and build up the body of Christ. These grace ministries will function until we all attain oneness into the faith, until we all experience the fullness of what it means to know the Son of God, and finally we become one into a perfect man with the full dimensions of spiritual maturity and fully developed into the abundance of Christ. And then our immaturity will end! And we will not be easily shaken by trouble, nor led astray by novel teachings or by the false doctrines of deceivers who teach clever lies.

This passage holds a lot of neat things, but the first one is that the goal is (1) that all the children of God would attain oneness in the faith, (2) that we would all experience the fullness of Christ, and (3) that we would be completely, fully spiritually mature. For us all to reach this level requires that we are all growing together and bringing one another along with us as we learn. The Lord's desire is that we would all be one and grow together, that we would all experience His never-ending riches, treasures, and benefits.

What is particularly neat about this idea in verse 13 is the extent of the words used. It says we will have become perfect, will have attained the full dimensions of spiritual maturity, and will be fully developed into the abundance of Christ. This is a "reaching the finish line" kind of completeness. This is not partial; it is 100 percent. But what is even neater is that in verse 14, it describes what the body of Christ will be like in that day. It says that we will no longer be immature, we will not be easily shaken by trouble, and we won't be led astray by novel teachings or false doctrines that do not come from God. This list implies that we are still on earth when we reach the ultimate fullness of Christ. There can't be false doctrines and troubles in heaven or thereafter. God has given us all of His fullness for us to fully and completely attain prior to heaven. He has given us to learn everything about Him in this lifetime. There is no part of Himself that He is withholding until a future time. He has given us all of Himself now. All we must do is seek Him out and let His love teach us.

We are coming into an era where we are all going to be discovering *every* dimension of God and will reach His ultimate fullness, and we will do it as one body. The Lord is ready for us to come into His fullness. He has prepared and made ready an era where we will reach what these verses speak of: the body of Christ finally made perfect in every way; to the point where in verse 13 it says that the five-fold ministry of apostles, prophets, evangelists, shepherds, and teachers will no longer be needed and will stop functioning because every one of us has been perfected in Christ. Get ready, because the Lord is sending us into a new era where we are going to attain all that He is and offers. Get ready!

ENDNOTES

Chapter 1

1 "Strong's Greek: 1380. Δοκέω (Dokeó)—to Have an Opinion, to Seem," n.d., https://biblehub.com/greek/1380.htm.

2 "2 Corinthians 3:9 Lexicon: For If the Ministry of Condemnation Has Glory, Much More Does the Ministry of Righteousness Abound in Glory.," n.d., https://biblehub.com/lexicon/2_corinthians/3-9.htm.

3 "Strong's Greek: 1380. Δοκέω (Dokeó)—to Have an Opinion, to Seem."

4 "Strong's Greek: 1380. Δοκέω (Dokeó)—to Have an Opinion, to Seem."

5 "Strong's Greek: 4053. Περισσός (Perissos)—Abundant," n.d., https://biblehub.com/greek/4053.htm.

Chapter 2

1 "Strong's Greek: 5485. Χάρις (Charis)—Grace, Kindness," n.d.,'/ https://biblehub.com/greek/5485.htm.

Chapter 3

[1] "Strong's Greek: 166. Αἰώνιος (Aiónios)—Agelong, Eternal," n.d., https://
biblehub.com/greek/166.htm.

[2] "2 Corinthians 3:9 Lexicon: For If the Ministry of Condemnation Has
Glory, Much More Does the Ministry of Righteousness Abound in Glory."
"Strong's Greek: 1380. Δοκέω (Dokeó)—to Have an Opinion, to Seem."

[3] "Strong's Greek: 1391. Δόξα (Doxa)—Opinion (Always Good in N.T.),
Hence Praise, Honor, Glory."

[4] "Strong's Greek: 1391. Δόξα (Doxa)—Opinion (Always Good in N.T.),
Hence Praise, Honor, Glory."

Chapter 4

[1] "2 Corinthians 3:9 Lexicon: For If the Ministry of Condemnation Has
Glory, Much More Does the Ministry of Righteousness Abound in Glory."

[2] "Strong's Greek: 1380. Δοκέω (Dokeó)—to Have an Opinion, to Seem."

[3] "Strong's Greek: 1380. Δοκέω (Dokeó)—to Have an Opinion, to Seem."

[4] "Strong's Greek: 1378. Δόγμα (Dogma)—an Opinion, (a Public) Decree,"
n.d., https://biblehub.com/greek/1378.htm.

Chapter 5

[1] "Asceticism Definition - Google Search," n.d., https://www.google.com/
search?q=asceticism+definition&sca_esv=594112619&rlz=1C1ONGR_
enUS1007US1007&sxsrf=AM9HkKnm2-1MCikJ9MAN3fboRyXcJlWW
UQ%3A1703725116605&ei=PMiMZcrHJJry0PEPsqCayAY&oq=
ascetesism&gs_lp=Egxnd3Mtd2l6LXNlcnAiCmFzY2V0ZXNpcm20q
AggBMgoQABiABBixAxgKMg0QABiABBiKBRhDGLEDMgcQABiA
BBgKMgcQABiABBgKMgcQABiABBgKMgcQABiABBgKMgcQABiA
BBgKMgcQABiABBgKMgcQABiABBgKMgcQABiABBgKSK4fUNQ
FWOETcAF4AZABAJgBxQGgGgAbwIqgEDNS41uAEByAEA-AEBqAIU

wgIHECMY6gIYJ8ICExAAGIAEGIoFGEMY6gIYtALYAQHCAg8QIxi
ABBiKBRgnGEYY-QHCAgoQIxiABBiKBRgnwgIXEC4YgAQYigUYkQ
IYsQMYgwEYxwEY0QPCAgsQABiABBiKBRiRAsICCxAAGIAEGLED
GIMBwgIREC4YgAQYsQMYgwEYxwEY0QPCAg4QLhiABBiKBRixAxi
DAcICCxAuGIAEGMcBGNEDwgIkEΛAYgAQYigUYRhj5ARiXBRiMBR
jdBBhGGPQDGPUDGPYD2AECwgIQEAAYgAQYigUYkQIYRhj5AcIC
ChAAGIAEGIoFGEPCAicQABiABBiKBRiRAhhGGPkBGJcFGIwFGN0
EGEYY9AMY9QMY9gPYAQLCAg4QABiABBiKBRiRAhixA8ICFhAu
GIAEGIoFGEMYsQMYgwEYxwEY0QPCAhMQABiABBiKBRiRAhix
AxhGGPkBwgIIEAAYgAQYsQPCAgUQABiABMICKhAAGIAEGIoF
GJECGLEDGEYY-QEYlwUYjAUY3QQYRhj0Axj1Axj2A9gBAsICDR
AAGIAEGLEDGLEDGArCAg0QABiABBixAxiDARgK4gMEG.

Chapter 7

[1] "Strong's Greek: 2540. Καιρός (Kairos)—Time, Season," n.d., https://biblehub.com/greek/2540.htm.

[2] "Strong's Greek: 553. Ἀπεκδέχομαι (Apekdechomai)—to Await Eagerly," n.d., https://biblehub.com/greek/553.htm.

[3] "Strong's Greek: 4983. Σῶμα (Sóma)—a Body," n.d., https://biblehub.com/greek/4983.htm.

[4] Bill Johnson Teaching (Official), "Discovering the Way of Life—Bill Johnson Devotional | The Pursuit of Wisdom, Sessions 1-4," December 20, 2023, https://www.youtube.com/watch?v=m5ZyUvowy6k.

ABOUT THE AUTHOR

Joanna Duell is a passionate lover of Jesus, and she enjoys spending time in the outdoors and gardening. She is currently a college student and a baker who loves to create her own recipes. She also enjoys playing and writing piano music. Joanna lives in Colorado with her family when she is not away at college.